S0-BYA-540

Airworthy!

Flying Vintage Aircraft

Airw

orthy!

Flying Vintage Aircraft

Ian S Mulelly Hugh R Smallwood

BLANDFORD PRESS
Poole   Dorset

First published in the U.K. 1981
by Blandford Press
Link House, West Street,
Poole, Dorset, BH15 1LL

Copyright © 1981 Ian S. Mulelly and
Hugh R. Smallwood

British Library Cataloguing in Publication Data

Mulelly, Ian
  Airworthy.
  1. Airplanes – Museums   2. Airplanes
  I. Title   II. Smallwood, Hugh

  629.133'34   TL506.A1

ISBN 0 7137 0966 9

All rights reserved. No part of this book may be
reproduced or transmitted in any form or by any means,
electronic or mechanical, including photocopying,
recording or any information storage and retrieval system,
without permission in writing from the Publisher.

Typeset in Monophoto 10/11 pt Garamond
Printed and bound in Great Britain by
Morrison & Gibb Ltd., London and Edinburgh

Title page

*Flt Lt Peter Gostick flying the RAF Battle of Britain
Memorial Flight's Hawker Hurricane Mk IIC shortly
after it was presented to the Flight by Hawker Siddeley
Aviation in April 1969. It is coded to represent the
aircraft of Sqn Ldr R S Tuck when he commanded No 257
Squadron.*

Contents

To the late Neil Williams

Introduction

Since their very beginning, aircraft have been at the forefront of scientific and technological development. As new materials, theories and techniques have been developed, the aircraft industry has taken them up. Indeed the process has also been reversed; many developments by the aircraft industry have now found their way into everyday life. This is typified by the many 'spin-offs' which have come from projects such as Concorde and the space programme.

However, just as aircraft have been pioneering technological development they have, at the same time, been the first to be discarded when the technology has become outdated. In fact, the process of innovation and invention has been so rapid that some aircraft have been obsolescent before they have gone into service. Until recently there has been very little conscious preservation of the machines which have played such an important part of life in the twentieth century. It is true that some aircraft have been put to one side for posterity and put on show in the draughty rafters of museums, but generally there has been little acknowledgement of the debt which present technology owes to the earlier machines. At least this was the case until recently. However, over fifty years ago in Britain, Richard Shuttleworth started a collection of vintage aircraft, although in those days many of the aircraft could not be termed vintage. However, the farsighted Richard established a collection which was committed to keeping its aircraft flying and it was many years before another organisation took up the challenge of keeping old aircraft in the air.

The reasons behind the other collections of flying vintage aeroplanes must be as various as the collections themselves, and the reasons why spectators go to see them are equally diverse. There is a nostalgia associated with many of the aircraft, especially those of World War II. For some it is the evocative sound of a Supermarine Spitfire's Merlin engine, or the ominous silhouette of an Avro Lancaster against the clouds, but this is not the only attraction. There is an appreciative following for the few aircraft of World War I which are still flying and which must be beyond the memory and life span of the vast majority of interested observers, many of whom were born well into the jet age.

The technology behind the majority of these aircraft is within the grasp of most people with a basic mechanical knowledge. However, soon after the advent of the jet aircraft, flying machines became so advanced that one can only marvel at their complexity. As far as the early aircraft are concerned,

the fact that they could rise into the air at all is impressive enough, but that they continue to do so today is nothing short of amazing.

Modern aircraft, even the relatively simple club aircraft, are aerodynamically sophisticated and mechanically reliable. They have to be and in Britain the Civil Aviation Authority (CAA) makes sure that they are. It is even said that they are easier to fly than a modern car is to drive. Certainly those pilots experienced with 'tail draggers' have been known to be somewhat uncharitable towards their 'tricycle only' counterparts. Many of these older machines are basic by comparison and yet they were leaders in their field at the time. At long last individuals, groups, collections and organisations are putting an incredible amount of time, effort, money and enthusiasm into getting vintage aeroplanes into the air. Impressive, but grounded, collections such as those of the Royal Air Force Museum, Hendon, or the Science Museum, in Britain, serve a valuable purpose, but for many the sight of a permanently grounded aircraft which could be made to fly is as sad a sight as an eagle in a cage would be to a naturalist.

This book is a tribute to those concerned with flying collections and their aircraft. The photographs are an attempt to show the aircraft as they appear to the public and with a few exceptions have been taken by the authors from the same vantage points available to everyone.

The choice of aircraft profiled in this book has been difficult. A thematic approach was possible, but too restrictive, and in the event the final selection is a combination of those aircraft which are either historically significant or took the authors' imaginations for one reason or another. There is one common factor about these aircraft, however: they all have a traceable and continuous history. The dividing line between a genuine original aircraft and a replica can be a very difficult one to draw, and many have their own strong views on the subject. In a way it is typified by the tale of the broom, which has been in existence for over a hundred years, but has had five new handles and ten new heads!

Some aircraft have been rebuilt so many times that they now contain far more new material than original, but there is a continuity which runs through their history which seems to make the aircraft a repaired original rather than a replica. There are two overriding criteria, firstly the engine should be of a type which is contemporary with the original aircraft and could have been fitted to it during its active service life, and secondly the airframe should have been built with materials and assembled by techniques which are not too anachronistic. It would be neither necessary nor desirable, however, to be too pedantic over such matters. A Sopwith Triplane is being built in Yorkshire, England, which will be a replica in the true sense of the word but it will differ from the original aircraft only by having been built some sixty years later. There are other 'replicas' flying which for various reasons have neither the original airframes nor the engines and thus do not fall within the scope of this book, for example, the Shuttleworth Collection's admirable Bristol Boxkite. Perhaps the overriding consideration should be that the aircraft should be in the 'spirit' of its original time.

The history of aviation is complicated and involved and has been covered many times from many points of view, and it is not our intention to condense it into a few pages. However, an attempt has been made to place the aircraft featured in this book into their historical perspective. The aircraft featured are presented in order of their construction.

The major part that warfare has played in the development of the aircraft is very obvious and quite understandable, although the original military use of aeroplanes was very tame, even passive, in comparison with modern usage. A more puzzling aspect of the aeroplane's history was the quite remarkable boom in civil aviation in the years immediately preceding and during the depression. In the post World War I era most nations were struggling to recover from the cost of the war, resources were in short supply, and especially as far as the working man was concerned, so was money; yet, while the western world was reeling under its worst financial crisis in history, the light-aircraft industry, after a period in the doldrums following the end of World War I, was flourishing. This was the era of great air races, barnstorming, flying circuses, de Havilland Moths, record breaking, and great deeds of aviation daring with apparently no military significance. But by the middle of the 1930s war was seen to be inevitable and the plans of many of the major aircraft of World War II which were laid down before the outbreak of hostilities benefitted greatly from the design experience gained in the 1920s.

Acknowledgements

The authors have tried, where time and money allowed, to research independently into the featured airworthy aircraft. This, however, was not always practicable and they are indebted to the help provided by the Putnam Publication books, especially A J Jackson's *British Civil Aircraft*. In addition virtually every other relevant book and publication (particularly *Vintage Aircraft Magazine* and *Aeroplane Monthly*) has been consulted. The greatest thanks, however, go to those individuals who have been so helpful in person, either over the telephone, or face to face. These, too numerous to mention, range from the Civil Aviation Authority's staff to aircraft owners, and from various forces' historical branches to the regular Old Warden commentator, Roger Hoefling. The authors are especially grateful to Harry Elkin and to Dick Richardson of the Strathallan Collection who provided the story of the Restoration of the Magister (which also appeared in *Vintage Aircraft Magazine* (No 2)) and the photographs. The majority of the photographs have been supplied by the authors, but we are especially grateful to Harry Elkin and Dick Richardson of the Strathallan Collection, John Batchelor, and Irene Smallwood, who have so kindly supplied further photographs and help. Thanks are also due to Bob Elliot of the Shuttleworth Collection Library, and to Michael O'Leary who has made an invaluable contribution in providing the photographs and histories of the American-based aeroplanes.

It is hoped that this book will be read in the spirit in which it was written. The heart of the book is the collection of airworthy aircraft histories. The authors have tried to be as accurate as possible but would be very grateful to hear from readers who can provide further information about aircraft featured.

Finally we must express our thanks to our wives and families who have travelled around patiently, and even interestedly, to the airshows over the last few years and given us the encouragement to continue with the venture.

Photograph Credits = (Colour in bold) Air Portraits Colour Library:– **33** (Bottom); **35** (Bottom); **37** (Bottom). John Batchelor:– 109. Harry Elkin:– 13–17, 20. Wilfred Hawkes:– **33** (Top); **35** (Top); Jim Larsen:– 106 (Top, Bottom). Michael O'Leary:– **71** (Top, Bottom); **73** (Top, Bottom); **79** (Top, Bottom); **93** (Top, Bottom). Ministry of Defence:– 2/3; 100. Richard E Richardson:– 21–27; **61** (Bottom); **63** (Bottom).

B–17 Ltd's Boeing B–17G Flying Fortress Sally B *banks steeply for the crowd at Old Warden after a typically spectacular low-level pass. One of the most remarkable features of the B–17's display is the quietness of the four Wright Cyclones on such a majestic aircraft.*

The Restoration of Vintage Aircraft - Two Case Studies

Every aircraft which undergoes restoration poses its own problems for the restorer. Things which would worry one owner, will be ignored by another, or might not even be cause for concern. Some restorers methodically bring all the components up to the fully restored condition, concurrently, whereas others fully restore one component, before moving on to the next. This, coupled with the number of workers available, and the time schedule, accounts for the major differences in restoration practice. Probably the biggest contrast in techniques in Britain is in the restoration of six Spitfires undertaken by Doug Arnold at Blackbushe, Surrey, and the restoration of the Nord 1101 by Harry Elkin at Denham, Buckinghamshire.

Doug Arnold has a team of full-time engineers and 'apprentices' led by Dick Melton, ex-Chief Engineer in the Royal Air Force's Battle of Britain Memorial Flight ground crew, whose work is supplemented by impeccable work done by volunteer enthusiasts.

The six Spitfires were lined up side by side on trestles in a new hangar, and were stripped and re-built more or less simultaneously. Each original magnesium rivet had to be drilled out and the airframe skin re-fixed with aluminium rivets in place of the magnesium ones which, although appearing to be sound (indeed, many Spitfires are still flying held together with these rivets), had, in fact, succumbed to corrosion. They were so weak that it was possible to snap away by hand the strengthening members held on with them. The Rolls-Royce Merlin engines for these aircraft are being serviced in the USA, where there are still engineers who are currently employed on servicing Merlins, and when necessary the airframes are X-rayed using portable equipment from Dan-Air.

The restoration being carried out by Harry Elkin, in his spare time, in a minute workshop on the edge of Denham airfield is in complete contrast. Yet, in the final analysis, it would be a brave man who would try to judge between the relative merits of the two restorations.

Doug Arnold's establishment is somewhat exceptional, so we have compared Harry Elkin's restoration with the work done by the full-time team of engineers at Strathallan who put a Miles Magister back into the air again after a lay-off of ten years. The two restorations are described not to enable com-

parative evaluation to be made, but to give some insight into the problems faced when restoring two very different aircraft in totally different circumstances, and how these problems are solved.

The chances of finding a wrecked or long-abandoned aircraft and getting it back into flying condition are very remote. Even those aircraft of World War II which have been discovered apparently free from corrosion or irreparable damage will require a phenomenal amount of work on them before any CAA inspector may be persuaded that they are safe enough to fly, and facilities will be required which are unlikely to be within the grasp of private individuals. Consequently very many of the vintage aircraft now flying have never been in a very advanced state of neglect and indeed some have never been grounded.

In Great Britain there is also the British Aircraft Preservation Council (BAPC), the representative agency which endeavours to co-ordinate and raise the standard of the work of British groups dedicated to preserving aircraft for future generations. Run by volunteers, it was formed in Derby in October 1967 from the Northern Aircraft Preservation Society

(now The Aeroplane Collection) whose members realised that the lack of communication between preservation groups inhibited pooling knowledge and information.

The BAPC now has over 70 member organisations throughout the UK. Membership is broadly based: any British organisation concerned with any aspect of aircraft preservation is eligble, including small specialist-groups who contribute invaluably to major projects, static museums, and groups dedicated to keeping historic aircraft airworthy, of both professional and amateur status (individuals are not eligible), producing cross-fertilisation and common-ground. Overseas organisations are associate members, resulting in a co-ordinated exchange of information and artifacts.

The BAPC's quarterly meetings are a forum for

Far left: Restoration of the fuselage of one of Doug Arnold's two ex-Indian air force Supermarine FR Mk XVIII Spitfires (here, G–BRAF/SM969/HS877).
Below: A Spitfire's starboard wing being restored, supervised by Dick Melton, Chief Engineer of Warbirds of Great Britain.

Above: *School leaver drilling corroded magnesium rivets from a structural component of a Spitfire, in the workshop of Warbirds of Great Britain at Blackbushe airport.*
Left: *Doug Arnold, owner of Warbirds of Great Britain, shows off a beautifully restored Spitfire port wing-tip, the work of volunteer helpers.*

the discussion of ideas and policy. There is a surprising consensus of opinion for such a diverse membership. Avoiding disciplinarian laws, the BAPC prefers a code of conduct between member organisations. While not an arbitrary body, the BAPC fosters links with the Press, aircraft industry and airlines. It has a loan fund to assist struggling member groups, helps find materials and specialist personnel, provides advice on many aspects of preservation, and has a library of technical books for consultation.

Nord 1101

Although the Bf 109 was the most famous Messerschmitt aircraft, and probably the most famous German aircraft ever built, perhaps the lesser known Bf 108 could claim to have been Willi Emil Messerschmitt's most successful design. In 1933 a contract for a light aircraft to take part in an air rally was given to Messerschmitt's company, the Bayerische Flugzeugwerke (BFW). The aircraft which emerged was a four-seater of all metal stressed skin construction with retractable main undercarriage wheels and a tail wheel. Known as the *Taifun* (Typhoon) it proved to be a great success and went on being improved over the next sixteen years. It was used for fast communication duties, ferrying, rescue, supply and target towing by both the *Luftwaffe* and civilian organisations. The design innovations which were pioneered on this aircraft and its variants were used on the legendary Bf 109.

One of the last modifications to which it was subjected was the substitution of a retractable nose wheel for the tail wheel. This aircraft was re-designated the Me 208 and two prototypes were built at the Les Mûreaux plant in France before the end of World War II, but one was destroyed in a bombing raid. After the war SNCA du Nord produced the Me 208 under the name Nord 1101, or Noralpha, at Les Mûreaux. They were used as advanced trainers and communication aircraft by the French *Armée de l'Air* and *Aéronavale*. Although considered to be a direct descendant of the Bf 108, the Me 208 is only superficially similar. There are no interchangeable parts of any significance and there are many totally different design details.

In 1946 Noralpha No 167 came off the production line and went into service. No details are available of its service record, but it appears that it was not used extensively and under 1000 hours had been recorded by the time it was 'civilianised' in 1965.

It came on to the market as F–BLQB and was

During the initial inspection of the Nord 1101 at Redhill in winter 1968 an attempt was made to set the propeller to fine pitch. The engine was then overhauled for the ferry flight to Denham.

acquired in late 1965 by Arnold Frutin and registered as G–ATJW. Some six months later it was sold to Keith Fenwich who flew it in silver livery for a couple of years, during which time it passed through the hands of Doug Bianchi at Booker, Buckinghamshire, who serviced it and arranged the renewal of its Certificate of Airworthiness (C of A). It came to rest at Redhill in Surrey; for some reason Mr Fenwich gave up flying it and it ended up in a corner of the airfield exposed to the ravages of the weather and local children.

In late 1968 it was discovered by Harry Elkin and its resurrection was assured. Harry is a professional industrial and scientific photographer working with Martin Baker of ejector seat fame. He learned to fly in the late 1950s in a de Havilland DH82 Tiger Moth at Reading, Berkshire, and later progressed to twin-engined aircraft. Aircraft restoration is not a new activity for him; in 1967 he and his friend, Edwin Harris, acquired a de Havilland DH94 Moth Minor which Harry re-built in a private workshop near Windsor, Berkshire. This impressive little aircraft is

The Nord 1101's instrument panel before restoration gives only an indication of the amount of restoration work that was required.

now part of the Strathallan Collection, at Auchterarder, Tayside, Scotland.

He came across the Nord whilst still flying the DH94 Moth Minor. It was in superficially poor condition, with four inches of water and a crop of mushrooms in the cabin; some of the fabric control surfaces had been torn and there was some sign of, perhaps, a heavy landing, for a panel covering under one of the fuel tanks and the wing inner panel had been buckled; the brakes also seemed to be non-functional.

Harry commuted between Redhill and Denham, Buckinghamshire, by car for a couple of weekends and gave the machine a thorough inspection. The main structural parts of the airframe seemed in surprisingly good condition and after a relatively small amount of work he managed to get the engine, a Le Rhône-built Renault 6Q10, going. It was

The cockpit of the Nord 1101 after removal of instrument panel, seats and primary controls, shows the extent of the deterioration.

obvious that No 6 cylinder was faulty. With his friend, Edwin Harris, Harry bought the aircraft for £250 and over the next five months he went to Redhill each weekend to restore it to a safe flying condition to get it back to Denham. The control surfaces were patched up, and the brakes repaired. The undercarriage was locked in the down position with jury struts, the engine stripped down and the faulty cylinder and valves were brought back to Denham for repair. Eventually it was ready and was allowed one flight under 'Condition A' (a temporary permit to fly granted by the CAA for the purpose of obtaining an airworthiness certificate or to enable an aircraft to get to a place for work to be done on it which will lead to it obtaining a certificate).

Harry had managed to do a circuit on a test flight of a similar aircraft in order to become familiar with the controls and so, on 28 May 1969, with the propeller locked in fine pitch, he flew it uneventfully back to Denham. He had been able to rent a small Nissen hut, no larger than a garage, at the back of Denham airfield, and here he started on the restoration which was to take him over two years. In order to get the aircraft into the hut, apart from any other reasons, he had first to remove the wings and the engine.

Structurally the machine was sound, so it was not stripped right down. The control surfaces were re-covered with fabric and the engine given a complete overhaul. The interior was cleared out and re-upholstered. The exterior silver paint was stripped off and the aircraft repainted in beige and black.

G–ATJW flew again in 1972 and proved to be a very impressive aeroplane. It went to the Jersey Air Rally in 1972 and won the 'Concours d'Elégance' as the best displayed aircraft in any class, and also the Decca Trophy for the best aircraft in its class (over ten years old). In 1973 it won the Decca Trophy and in 1972, 1973 and 1974 won 'Quennevais' awards for navigation.

In 1970 Harry heard of a new Hispano/Renault

The fully restored instrument panel after the instruments have been factory-overhauled and re-calibrated.

6Q10 engine at Romans St Paul in France. He flew the Moth Minor across the Channel and then flew in a further four and a half hour hop down to Romans, to have a look at the engine. He continued the journey to St Raphäel, near Cannes, flew into some bad weather and had to make a precautionary landing in a field 1200 m (4000 ft) up in the mountains to wait all night for the weather to improve. Some time later Harry borrowed a Ford Transit van and drove non-stop to Romans to pick the engine up. It had been bought, still in its crate, from the French Navy, by a group of enthusiasts, intending to put it in a racing aircraft. This was never built so they sold it to Harry for what they paid for it — £80. They have now become close friends and he returns each year to help them sample the new local wine.

Even getting the engine back to Britain posed problems. The crate was too big to go in the van, so the engine had to be uncrated and at the risk of multiple hernias, six of them just managed to get it into the van. After a two-day journey back to the coast they arrived at the harbour in a thunderstorm.

The French official, on inspecting the customs docket, assumed that the 'Renault Engine' was a car engine. As it had cost only £80 it had been entered as having no commercial value and consequently he refused to venture into the rain to inspect it. On the other side of the Channel, however, the British customs officers were not so happy about the 'unapproved' import of an aircraft engine and impounded it. A week later it was released for the additional sum of £12. Although the original engine was still serviceable, it was changed in 1974 for the new one.

Importing aircraft parts seems to create quite unusual problems. It was rumoured that a new propeller was available at Cannes. Harry sent a cheque to an acquaintance near there to pass on to the owner to clinch the deal, but unfortunately it turned out to be a 'cash only' transaction. However, for £60

The interior of the Nord 1101's fuselage looking aft, after it had been painstakingly rebuilt and etch-chromated against corrosion.

it was too good a chance to miss. He flew out with a friend in their Wassmer Baladou, but en route they flew into a storm and on emerging from it the aircraft didn't feel too reliable. So they decided to land, only to discover that the storm had uncovered an illegal and previously undiscovered repair done with tarred paper, and beneath it the ribs and struts were rattling around loose. The aircraft had to be abandoned and, in fact, took six months to be re-built by the Wassmer factory at Issoire. They continued by train and taxi and picked up the six foot long propeller in Cannes. No-one seemed prepared to offer a lift back to the railway station to a pair with a heavy, unwieldy propeller resting across their shoulders like a coffin, so having footed it some way along the road, Harry sat down on the verge and eventually removed one of the blades from the boss. This made the thing less conspicuous and eventually they were given a lift into

the station. The two blades were strapped together making it relatively compact, but French railway regulations were such that it had to travel in a goods truck. That was the last they saw of it for six months. When they arrived at their destination it was not to be found. Luckily they had written the address of the Wassmer factory on it, and six months later, Harry flew the Nord 1101 back to France with the owner of the Baladou to pick it up following the re-build, and the propeller was waiting for them there.

The gradual increase in the price of fuel eventually persuaded Harry that the time had come to ground 'Juliet Whisky' and do a complete re-build in the hope that by the time it was finished fuel matters might have improved. The last flight was in November 1976 when he flew to Strathallan to pick up the crew who were delivering the BA Swallow 2 (G–ADPS) to Sir William Roberts' collection.

Harry then spent two evenings a week and most Sundays in the workshop at the back of Denham airfield restoring the Nord to immaculate condition. He works slowly and methodically, no job is rushed,

and there is no sense of impatience about the work.

He started by removing the engine and then worked back along the aircraft from the firewall. Each removable piece of metal was taken off, cleaned and stripped back to the bare metal. Chemical paint removers can cause additional corrosion if not quickly neutralised, so this method was used only for large surface areas, where there were no cracks for the liquid to run into; for the rest it was laborious work. Using a wire brush on an electric drill was ruled out because there is too great a risk of damaging the metal. The number of repairs was quite small, but minor bumps and dents were smoothed out or filled in. There was very little corrosion of the metal. One area which had suffered was the inside wing by the centre rib; the control rod for the ailerons emerges through a small rectangular hole towards the trailing edge of the wing and, presumably, this had allowed the ingress of moisture.

The corroded areas were treated with 'Deoxidine' which 'kills' the corrosion. In this process, after the Deoxidine has been cleaned off, the metal is etch-

Harry Elkin removing a local patch of corrosion from one of the Nord's wings with a hand-tool, at his workshop at Denham airfield.

chromated, as is the rest of the bare metal. This coats the metal in a matt yellow-green covering which is to be seen on most aircraft undergoing repair or restoration. It protects the metal from further corrosion and, for the outer surfaces, provides a good key for subsequent coats of paint.

Outer surfaces of the Nord have two coats of painstakingly applied polyurethane paint, every drop being filtered immediately prior to being sprayed or brushed on, giving a perfect final finish. All the nuts and bolts were cleaned and if necessary re-plated and stress-relieved, and the light alloy fittings were re-anodised.

The cabin was once again stripped out though this time the seats did not need attention. All the instruments were removed and sent to 'Pandit' of High Wycombe for servicing and re-calibrating; this was one of the major expenses of the restoration.

The completely restored fuselage of the Nord 1101, already painted, demonstrates Harry's policy of discrete, total restoration of components.

Over the years Harry has made many friends and contacts who have been able to help him on small matters and hardly any component of the aeroplane has had to be completely replaced, which would have made the job much more expensive. The real cost of the restoration has been Harry's time which as yet he has not dared to add up. He philosophically writes this off as 'a labour of love'.

The centre inboard section of the wing had to be unriveted so that repairs could be made internally in a section which is normally sealed. The metal skin is strengthened by wood in places where it is used as a walkway or step; these had eventually rotted away and needed replacing. Rubber seals had to be replaced and some of these were able to be matched 'off the shelf' from James Walker Limited. The brakes were re-lined by Mintex, and a windscreen was replaced.

The aircraft was inspected at every major stage, for instance when the wings were to be assembled, by a friend who is an engineer. The CAA inspector called on an informal basis every now and then to see how the work was progressing, but an official inspection had to be made when all the work had been completed and before any significant areas were sealed up permanently.

The new colour scheme is as close as Harry can get to the machine's original *Aéronavale* colours of dark blue upper surfaces and duck egg blue lower surfaces, and showing the crescent and star insignia of 3F (*Troisiéme Flotille* — No 3 Squadron). He was persuaded to do this by the late Doug Bianchi during their many chats about restoring the aircraft and the final scheme was taken out of a book on French naval aircraft. The French Navy have given permission for its colours to be used, but although sympathetic, they could not provide any details of its service history.

It is a sad postscript that the cost of fuel has now increased so much that although the aircraft is finished and virtually ready to fly, it is unlikely to grace the skies for some time. Since it last flew the

Above: *Harry Elkin's Nord 1101 flying after its first restoration and wearing the colour scheme with which it won the* Concours d'Elégance *at the Jersey Air Rally in 1972.*
Right: *An unusual angle on the Nord 1101's Renault 6QT inverted six-cylinder engine, seen with the cylinder head and block removed.*

cost of filling its tank has gone up sevenfold and despite requests for it to appear in air shows it would be flown so rarely in between times that it is going to be kept in storage rather than let the elements get at it again. Of course, if any enthusiast has a spare £25,000 and a hankering for a Messerschmitt they might like to contact Harry!

Miles M.14 Magister

Harry Elkin twice restored the Nord in a small workshop at the back of an airfield, working on his own in his spare time, but restoring such aircraft generally requires facilities and experience not often available to one individual. Thus, many — but certainly not all — of the vintage aircraft flying today have been restored by organisations, notably the Shuttleworth Collection at Old Warden, Bedfordshire, the Strathallan Collection at Auchterarder, Tayside, Scotland, and the Duxford Aviation Society, Cambridgeshire; the Confederate Air Force, Texas, and the Old Rhinebeck Museum, New York. Mention must also be made of Personal Planes Services at Booker, Buckinghamshire, which, originally under the leadership of the late Doug Bianchi, and now of his son Tony, restores, cossets and generally ministers unto many vintage aircraft owned by individuals.

In contrast to the Nord, an all-metal, side-by-side advanced training aircraft, it is interesting to look at the restoration of the Strathallan Miles M.14 Magister, a mainly spruce and plywood built, tandem seat basic trainer. It was restored by an organisation with a relatively large amount of room, full time engineers and technicians and a wealth of expertise and facilities, although all this does not necessarily make restoration easy.

The 'Maggie' in question, R1914, was built in 1939 by Phillips and Powis Aircraft Limited at Woodley, Berkshire (c/n 1900), and first flew in the November of that year. It joined No 604 Squadron, RAF, in November 1940, and later spent time in various Maintenance Units and for a month was on loan to No 137 Squadron. By the end of World War II it was in storage with 5 MU having completed only 309 flying hours. 'Civilianised' in 1946 it became 'Hawk Trainer III', G–AHUJ, and joined the Loch Leven Aero Club at Balado. When the club folded up, the McDonald Aircraft Company took it over and stored

The Miles M.14 Magister being secured to the truck on which it made its journey from Jim Smith's garage in Cults, Aberdeenshire to Auchterarder, Perthshire, in February 1975.

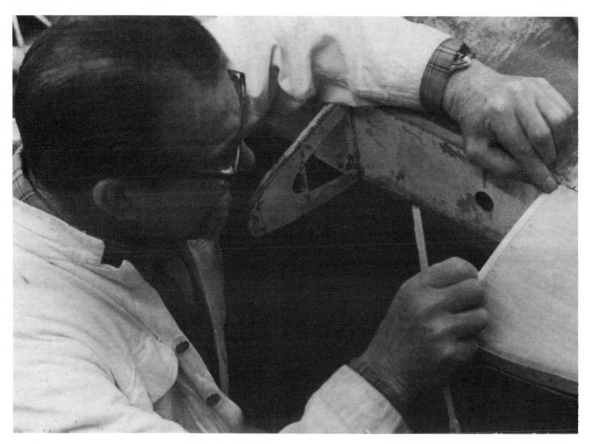

it until March 1951 when Stewart Henderson and his son discovered it in a pool of water surrounded by Fairey Barracudas which were awaiting the axe. The machine was in good condition and changed hands for £100. Stewart Henderson first flew her in April 1951 and subsequently he and his son logged over 400 hours of apparently idyllic flying over the Perthshire hills. In 1964 Jim Russell of Aberdeen acquired the aircraft, but a year later he left Scotland for Kuwait. He took the precaution of inhibiting the engine and it remained in storage until 1975. Taken over by the Strathallan Collection, it was moved from Jim's garage at his house in Cults, Aberdeenshire, to the Collection in February 1975.

Jim Smith, Strathallan's chief engineer, examined the machine and concluded that refurbishing would be straightforward, but would take a long time. In fact, it had its first flight sixteen months later. The engine, a Gipsy Major 1f, was removed and put in an engine stand to facilitate a 'top end' overhaul. It was in excellent condition thanks to the precautions taken by Jim Russell ten years earlier. The work on the

Above: *Jim Smith working on the leading edge of the Magister's wing-tip, in December 1975, Damaged by water during storage three new ribs had to be manufactured and new plywood skinning applied. This was then finished off with cotton and red dope.*

Top right: *Installation of the Magister's immaculately restored Gipsy Major 1F engine.*

Right: *Jim Smith and Derek Barnes passing the aileron control cables through the wing prior to attachment to the centre-section.*

engine was done by Strathallan engineer David Lawson and, apart from looking like a new engine, it runs faultlessly.

The fuselage was completely stripped of all fittings, although the plywood covering was left on. Meanwhile, another team of engineers stripped the fabric-covered tail surfaces and prepared the internal members for re-covering. A few minor repairs were needed, but thanks to the use of 'Duralac' none of the steel parts of the hinges had corroded. The tail surfaces were then re-covered with Irish linen and red tautening dope.

In general, the wood and glue parts of the airframe had survived very well. The only section needing special attention was one wing tip which obviously had been soaked during storage. The plywood covering was removed and, as suspected, some of the ribs had deteriorated. Three new ones were manu-factured and fitted, a new plywood surface was put over them and the top was covered by 'grade A' cotton and red dope.

The undercarriage was stripped and, as in the Nord

Above: Fitting the wings back onto the Magister at Strathallan airfield, in the shadow of the port Rolls-Royce Merlin of the Collection's de Havilland Mosquito T Mk 35.

Top right: Port centre-section wing stub with the ten gallon fuel tank installed following the fuel tank pessure check.

Right: The Magister, fully restored, awaits the application of its RAF roundels and fin stripes. Note the anti-spin strake on the fuselage forward of the tailplane, a modifi-cation also applied by the RAF to their Tiger Moths.

Overleaf: The 1939 Magister Mk I sporting its authentic wartime livery, photographed near Strathallan airfield on its first flight test, 26 June 1976.

restoration, new oleo seals had to be fitted; in this case they were specially made by Lockheed at Speke.

Again 'Duralac' had done its job and the wing attachment fittings and bolts were in good condition. The fuel tanks had not suffered either, as pressure testing showed. They were repainted before refitting.

The instruments, again like those of the Nord, were stripped out and sent away for servicing, and on their return they were installed in new, matt black instrument panels. The flying control fittings were refurbished, and the vacuum tanks for the flap controls were pressure tested before being re-installed. The whole of the interior of the fuselage was painted in Interior Green cellulose paint which gives the machine a truly 'vintage' aroma.

The flying control cables which by now had been re-protected with lanolin resin, were installed in the fuselage and the machine was then ready for the fitting of the wings, a task performed by a large team of engineers after which all the controls were linked up. The propeller was fitted and by May 1976 satisfactory engine runs had been carried out and R1914 was ready for its final paint job. There is an interesting comparison here with the Nord: there, Harry Elkin completed each part of the machine before moving on to the next and this included

putting on the final coats of paint.

The final colour scheme for the 'Maggie' was supplied by Gill Wallace of Stewarton, Ayrshire, who is a specialist in such matters. The upper surfaces are camouflaged in Dark Green and Dark Earth; the under surfaces are Training Yellow. It differs from the only other airworthy Magister, P6382, flown by the Shuttleworth Collection, in having a camouflaged rudder (P6382 has a yellow one). The Shuttleworth 'Maggie' also has a curious dorsal, pale green diamond, which was supposed to give ground crews advance warning during World War II that mustard gas had been released.

David Ogilvy, the general manager of the Shuttleworth Collection, often seen piloting their 'Maggie', sent some pilot's notes to Bernie Sedgwick, a British Caledonian pilot who was to fly R1914. Not that Sedgwick was a stranger to them, as he had been an RAF Central Flying School instructor on the type. Thus on 26 June 1976, Bernie, accompanied by Derek Barnes, as flight engineer, took the Strathallan Magister into the air, returning thirty minutes later, grinning from ear to ear. The Magister was perfect; no problems had been met and no adjustments were needed. The number of flying Magisters in the world immediately doubled.

Airworthy Aircraft

Left: *The other airworthy Magister, of the Shuttleworth Collection, P6382. On the upper fuselage is a gas-attack warning triangle.*

The Confederate Air Force's Curtiss P-40N, N1226N, featured later in this section.

Aircraft Data

TYPE AND MARK	SERIAL AND REG. Nos.	YEAR OF MANUFACTURE	MANUFACTURER	CONSTRUCTION No. (C/N)	POWERPLANT	SPAN ft in	LENGTH ft in
Blériot Type IX	BAPC – 3	1909	Humber Co.	14?	22hp Anzani Fan	28 0	25 0
Deperdussin 1910 Monoplane	BAPC – 4	1910	Deperdussin	043?	35hp Anzani Y	28 9	27 6
Blackburn Type D Monoplane	BAPC – 5	1912	Blackburn	–	50hp Gnome	38 0	28 0
Luftverkers-Gessellschaft (LVG) C VI	7198/18	1917	LVG	–	230hp Benz BZ IX/BZ IV	44 8½	26 7½
Avro 504K	E3404, G – ADEV	1918	Avro	–	110hp Le Rhône	36 0	29 5
Royal Aircraft Factory SE5A	F – 904, G – EBIA	1918	Royal Aircraft Factory	654	200hp Wolseley W.4A Viper	26 7	20 11
Bristol F2B Fighter	D – 8096, G – AEPH	1918	Bristol	7575	275hp Rolls-Royce Falcon III	39 3	25 10
Sopwith Pup	G – EBKY, N5184, N5180	1920	Sopwith	W/o 3004/14	80hp Le Rhône	26 6	19 4
de Havilland DH51	G – KAA, VP – KAA, G – EBIR	1923	de Havilland	102	140hp Airdisco 120	37 0	26 6
Hawker Tomtit	K1786, G – AFTA	1928	Hawker	30380	150hp Armstrong Siddeley Mongoose	28 6	23 8
Comper CLA.7 Swift	VT – ADO, G – ACTF	1932	Comper	532/9	95hp Pobjoy Niagara	24 0	17 8½
Percival Type E2 Mew Gull	ZS – AHM, G – AEXF	1936	Percival	E – 22	210hp Gipsy Queen III	24 0	20 3
Gloster Gladiator Mk I	K8032, L8032, G – AMRK	1938	Gloster	–	840hp Bristol Mercury IX	32 3	27 5
Boeing Stearman A75N1 Kaydet	75-4775, G – AROY	1938	Boeing	–	450hp Pratt & Whitney R985AN/1 Wasp Junior	32 2	25 0
General Aircraft GAL 42 Cygnet	ES915, G – AGBN	1941	General Aircraft	111	2 × 150hp Blackburn Cirrus Major II	36 6	24 3
Hawker Hurricane Mk IIB	5588, G – AWLW, CF – SMI	1942	Canadian Car & Foundry Ltd.	–	1,635hp Rolls-Royce Merlin 25	40 0	32 2
Fairey Swordfish Mk II	LS326, G – AJVH	1943	Blackburn	–	750hp Bristol Pegasus 30	45 6	36 1
Douglas A – 26C Invader	43 – 22612, N3710G	1943	Douglas	–	2 × 2,000hp Pratt & Whitney R – 2800-79 Double Wasp	70 0	50 9
Vickers-Supermarine Spitfire LF Mk IXb	MH434, H – 105, H – 68, B – 15, SM – 41, OO – ARA, G – ASJV	1943	Vickers Armstrong	CBAF IX 552	1,720hp Rolls-Royce Merlin 76	36 10	31 1
Curtiss P – 40N – 5 Kittyhawk	867 (RCAF), N1226N	1944	Curtiss	–	1,200hp Allison V – 1710	37 4	33 4
North American P-51D – 25 – NA Mustang	NL32FF, NL2151D, W414237	1944	North American	30606	1,490hp Packard V – 1670 – 7 Merlin	37 0	32 3
North American TB – 25N Mitchell	44 – 30925, N9494Z	1944	North American	108 – 34200	2 × 1,850hp Wright R – 2600 – 29 Double Cyclone	67 7	52 11
Boeing B – 17G Fortress	44 – 85784, F – BGSR, N17TE	1944	Lockheed (Vega)	–	4 × 1,200hp Wright R – 1820 – 65 Cyclone	103 9	74 4
Republic P – 47N Thunderbolt	45 – 3436, 71 (Nicaragua) N478C, N47TB	1945	Republic	–	2,800hp Pratt & Whitney R – 2800 Double Wasp	42 7	36 1
de Havilland Mosquito T Mk 3	RR299, G – ASKH	1945	de Havilland	–	2 × 1,460hp Rolls-Royce Merlin	54 2	40 6
Nord 1002 Pingouin	F – OTAN – 5, F – BGVX, G – ATBG	1945	SNCA du Nord	121	233hp Renault 6Q10	34 5	28 1
Avro Lancaster B Mk I	PA474	1945	Vickers Armstrong	Contract No. A/c 2791	4 × 1,610hp Rolls-Royce Merlin 24	102 0	69 6
Hawker Sea Fury FB Mk 11	TF956	1946	Hawker	–	2,480hp Bristol Centaurus 18	38 5	34 8
Miles M.65 Gemini IA	OO – CDO, G – AKKH	1947	Miles	6479	2 × 100hp Blackburn Cirrus Minor II	36 2	22 3
Fairey Firefly AS Mk 5	WB271	1949	Fairey	–	2,250hp Rolls-Royce Griffon (5)74	41 2	37 11
Chance Vought F4U – 7 Corsair	N33714	1952	Chance Vought	Bu. No. 133714	2,450hp Pratt & Whitney R – 2800 – 18W Double Wasp	41 0	34 6½
Yakovlev Yak – 11	OK – WIE, G – AYAK	?	Strojviny Privni Petiletsky	172701	730hp Shvetsov ASh 21	30 10	27 10

HEIGHT ft in	TARE/ALL-UP WEIGHT (lbs)	MAX. SPEED mph	CRUISING SPEED mph	RATE OF CLIMB ft/min	SERVICE CEILING ft	RANGE miles	ARMAMENT (as built)	CREW SEATS	NOTES
—	484/715	40	—	—	—	—	None	1	Possibly built under licence
—	500/ —	55	—	—	—	—	None	1	—
—	— /1,400	60	—	—	—	—	None	1	Original engine No. 776; present engine No. 683
10 4	2,090/3,058	118	—	—	21,325	410	2 × 7.92mm MG, 240lbs bombs	2	
10 5	1,231/1,829	90	78	—	16,000	250	1 × 0.303-in MG	1	Spurious E3404 Serial; Registration G – ADEV uncertain
9 6	1,531/1,940	120	—	1,175	19,500	300	2 × 0.303-in MG	1	—
9 9	1,930/2,800	125	—	1,200	19,500	350	2 × 0.303-in MG	2	—
9 6	787/1,225	110	—	1,090	17,500	310	1 × 0.303-in MG	1	Built as Dove; Spurious N5180 Serial
10 0	1,342/2,240	—	90	—	—	350	None	2	—
8 8	1,100/2,100	124	105	1,000	19,500	350	None	2	—
5 3½	540/985	140	120	1,400	22,000	380	None	1	Replacement engine: performance details for Pobjoy R
6 10	1,150/2,125	—	—	—	—	—	None	1	—
10 4	3,476/4,750	253	—	2,300	33,000	440	4 × 0.303-in MG	1	Composite aircraft
9 2	1,936/3,000	*125	*80	—	—	*300	None	1	*Much modified; details do not apply
5 10	1,200/1,900	150	128	850	17,000	650	None	2	—
13 1	5,640/7,800	340	—	2,700	35,600	700	12 × 0.303-in MG	1	Not original engine type
12 4	4,700/7,510	138	104 – 129	1,200	19,250	516	1 × 0.303-in MG, torpedo, rockets, or depth bombs	3	—
18 6	22,370/35,000	425	—	1,380	21,800	1,780	18 × 0.5-in MG, 4,000lbs bombs	3	—
12 7¾	5,610/9,500	404	324	4,100	43,000	200	2 × 20mm cannon, 4 × 0.303-in MG 1,000lbs bombs	1	Non standard engine. Also with clipped wings (span 32ft 2in); B armament
12 4	6,700/8,850	343	—	2,120	31,000	340	4/6 0.5-in MG 1,000lbs bombs	1	P – 40L Q.E.C. (Quick Engine Change) & Replacement engine + prop
13 8	7,125/11,600	437	—	3,475	41,900	950	6 × 0.5-in MG 10 rockets, 2,000lbs bombs	1	W414237 is spurious serial
16 4	21,100/35,000	275	—	1,100	24,000	1,500	13 × 0.5-in MG 4,000lbs bombs	6	—
19 1	31,150/65,500	287	210	—	35,600	2,000	13 × 0.5-in MG 6,000 – 12,800lbs bombs	10	Turrets missing
14 8	10,700/21,200	467	—	2,800	43,000	800	8 × 0.5-in MG 2,500lbs bombs or rockets	1	—
15 3½	14,100/17,500	380	300	1,750	34,000	1,860	None	2	One engine replaced, both de-rated
—	1,980/3,270	188	165	1,180	16,400	530	None	4	Not original engine
20 0	36,900/68,000	281	210	—	23,500	2,695	10 × 0.303-in MG 14,000lbs bombs	7	—
15 10	8,977/12,500	460	—	4,320	36,000	760	4 × 20mm cannon 2,000lbs bombs or rockets	1	—
7 6	1,910/3,000	145	135	650	13,500	820	None	4	—
14 4	9,674/14,000	386	—	2,000	28,400	660	4 × 20mm cannon 2,000lbs bombs	2	Engine modified
14 9¼	9,900/13,420	450	—	4,800	NA	1,000	4 × 20mm cannon 10 rockets, 4,000lbs bombs	1	—
—	4,410/5,500	263	286	—	—	795	None	2	—

Blériot Type IX

Louis Blériot's historic Channel flight, on 23 July 1909, was the result of courage, determination and the triumph of luck over adversities, but it might be suggested that the aircraft itself did not really warrant the acclaim that it was given at the time. It has been said that no pilot at the time, no matter how good, could have repeated the flight with the same machine and engine, and although about a year later de Lesseps flew a Blériot across the Channel to become the second man to make the crossing, this machine had been fitted with a 50hp Gnome rotary engine, instead of Louis Blériot's 22hp Anzani. However, Blériot's triumph over what amounted to a psychological barrier immediately resulted in orders for one hundred aircraft and brought him out of the ranks of the early pioneers to the very forefront, comparable even with the Wright brothers.

The Shuttleworth Blériot Type XI is identical to the one which made the first cross-Channel heavier-than-air flight. The design had been begun in late 1908 and it has been suggested that Raymond Saulnier played a major part in it. Originally it should have had a 30hp REP (Robert Esnault-Pelterie) engine driving a four-blade propeller. However, the engine was quickly replaced by the 22hp Anzani engine and a two-blade propeller. Control is achieved by a rudder (but there is no fin) and elevators, and wing warping for lateral control. The engine power is controlled by an 'ignition advance and retard lever', which is used as a primitive throttle control. In common with many other engines, lubrication is by a total loss castor oil system, fed to the engine by a pressurised tank. The pressure is generated from a pump operated by the pilot, though few flights these days require the pilot to operate the pump in flight.

The Shuttleworth Collection's Blériot is believed to be the fourteenth built and thought to have been one of the originals used by the Blériot school at Hendon which opened in 1910. It is assumed that it was built by the Humber Company under licence in England, as it was their pilot, Mr George Barns, who delivered it. In 1912 the aircraft crashed and was scrapped. It was found by a Mr A E Grimmer, being offered for sale by a waste merchant who had it stored under Blackfriars Railway Bridge in London. Mr Grimmer had nurtured a desire to fly for some years and, like many others since, buying and repairing a wrecked aeroplane was the cheapest way of achieving this end.

The aircraft was ready for its first flight on Easter Monday 1913, and it made a short hop on 'Postern Piece' in Bedfordshire. Later, it was moved to a Polo ground near Bedford where it was regularly flown, but only in straight lines. It was whilst flying here that Mr Grimmer landed somewhat suddenly when the port side cylinder blew off, ripping through the wing! On another occasion he found himself flying backwards when a strong headwind caught the aircraft as it lifted over a hedge.

A local retired builder reckoned that he could make a propeller for the 22hp Anzani engine which would make it fly at 200mph, and, indeed, at his own expense, he made one; but, before the engine had even reached half power the propeller fell apart! Some time later, in 1914, Mr Grimmer graduated to a Deperdussin.

The Blériot remained in storage until 1935 when Richard Shuttleworth was given custody of it. It was more or less completely re-built by the Collection. The Blériot never made much more than straight hops within the bounds of the airfield and then often only when the conditions were absolutely perfect. At the end of the July flying day in 1977, Neil Williams, in what turned out to be one of his last public flights at Old Warden, felt confident enough to try to do a complete circuit. The machine lifted over the hedge and rose as it encountered a thermal coming up from the cornfield. He slowly turned right, but as the aircraft went behind some trees it lost lift and nose-dived into a wire fence. Neil was unhurt, and some time later the remains of the aircraft were brought back across the airfield on the back of the Shuttleworth Morris 1000 pick-up.

Roger Hoefling, the regular Old Warden commentator, put out an immediate appeal for financial help, and before the last of the spectators had left, over £200 had been collected. The Blériot had to take its place with the rest of the machines needing restoration but, fortunately, the wings suffered little damage in the crash.

Right: *Shuttleworth's Blériot Type XI has now been completely rebuilt, and engine runs initiated. During the rebuild the tailwheel has been replaced by a skid, in keeping with earlier models.*

Deperdussin 1910 Monoplane

In the enthusiastic years following the Channel flight there was a great need for a rugged, reliable machine for training the would-be pilots, and among the many aircraft which were designed then was the Blériot-influenced Deperdussin. Sometimes referred to as the Monoplane (not to be confused with the successful 200km/ph racing aircraft of 1912), this aircraft could be bought for about £460, fitted with a 35hp Anzani three-cylinder radial (or 'Y') engine, and was used by most of the flying schools in Europe. Sometimes the aircraft was demonstrated at airshows or flown in races, but for such prestigious occasions the engine was replaced, probably by the ubiquitous 50hp Gnome rotary and sometimes by the 100hp version. Seeing the sedate Shuttleworth Collection's Anzani-powered Deperdussin it is difficult to believe that similar aircraft once held the world speed record.

The Shuttleworth aeroplane had been used for training purposes at Hendon, and later owned by a juggler whose 'party trick' was to drop eggs on his friends as he flew over them. The airport authorities had cause to impound the machine because of unpaid bills and whilst trying to break into the hangar, its owner pushed over a heavy door which fell onto it. It was put up for sale and bought in 1914 by the resourceful Mr A E Grimmer, who by then was becoming frustrated with the low powered Blériot.

Rudimentary woodwork and 'Croyd' glue enabled the machine to be repaired, and in those carefree days before the CAA inspectors, it was soon airworthy again and it was not long before Mr Grimmer felt confident enough to try a complete circuit.

With the outbreak of World War I, restrictions on private flying were imposed and the local policeman asked Mr Grimmer to stop flying; not to be put off he contacted the Home Office and persuaded them that as an engineer he was in a position to do valuable research into machine design and when the time came could help train 'our boys'. He was granted a permit to fly within three miles of the Polo field which he used as his base.

One day, while passing the Polo ground in his car, he was persuaded by his passengers to give a demonstration flight. It was a gusty day and against his better judgement Mr Grimmer took the machine up and did a circuit. As he came over a tree the plane took a nose-dive and hit the ground so hard that the wings were buried in the ground.

Being a motor engineer the damage to the engine posed few problems to Mr Grimmer, and Nicholls of Bedford made a new set of wings. Other pressures, however, brought on by the developing war, caused him to give up and the machine remained in this semi-repaired state until he gave it, along with the Blériot, to Richard Shuttleworth. The offer was made when the two of them met at a meeting held to debate the possibility of Bedford Municipal Airport in 1935.

The machine by then was in such poor condition that it needed to be re-built completely and re-covered, and the engine overhauled. The job was finished in 1937 and the machine was flown by Mr Shuttleworth.

In 1965 the aircraft was subjected to extensive repair and renovation. As with the other 'pioneer' aircraft in the Collection, it can only be flown on very still days and in practice this means in the evenings at the end of one of the airshows, but it is well worth staying to see it. The pilot nowadays is usually John Lewis, and gradually, hop by hop, the 'plane is being put through its paces. Practice times are very infrequent and, bearing in mind what happened to the Blériot, it is very unlikely that a complete circuit will be made, but it is hoped that it will be kept 'hopping' for many years to come.

Like the majority of the Shuttleworth Collection's aircraft, its Deperdussin 1910 Monoplane is the sole surviving airworthy example in the world. It is BAPC-4 on the British Aircraft Preservation Council's register, which was set up to assist historians and enthusiasts by providing an identity for aircraft which do not qualify for a service serial or a civil registration. Over 120 aircraft have been listed.

Blackburn Type D Monoplane 1912

This aircraft is still referred to as the Blackburn Monoplane and its origins were a little vague. However, thanks to the discovery of one of Blackburn's account books by Mr Byrne of Blackburns, now British Aerospace, and some detective work by A J Jackson, it is now known that this aircraft is a Type D originally fitted with engine No 776 and was built for a Mr Cyril Foggin by Blackburns in 1912. Inside the cockpit is a brass plate which proclaims the aircraft to be a Type B fitted with engine No 725. This plate is now known to have originated with a Hendon School machine. These early Blackburn machines were all 'one-offs' and were all unique. Mr Foggin, who had learnt to fly at the Blackburn School at Hendon, used the Type D machine in the Leeds area and it is known that it gave various exhibitions. On 2 June 1913 Mr Foggin sold it back to Robert Blackburn and the following day it was resold to Mr F Glew of Wittering, Wansworth, Northants. Its subsequent history is a little vague, although it seems to have been used in the Lincolnshire area. In 1914 it had a heavy landing and was abandoned. It was rediscovered in 1938 in a barn at Wittering and Richard Shuttleworth acquired it and started the process leading to its restoration.

Restoration was started in the early days of World War II, and completed in 1947. Since then the aircraft has been flying very regularly, though it has been back to Blackburn for some work to be done on it since then.

In these early days, every aircraft built was unique, and this one was no exception. In many ways it followed the design of the earlier 'Mercury' aeroplanes, although immediately before this a 70hp Renault-powered two-seater had been made, the military Type E of 1912, which was the first British aircraft to have a metal fuselage, but was too heavy to leave the ground. An earlier 'Mercury' had also been used for air-to-ground radio demonstrations.

The engine is a 50hp Gnome rotary, which had a considerable impact on the aviation scene when it appeared in 1909. It is partially cowled and this gives the Blackburn its characteristic appearance. This cowling is probably as much for protecting the pilot from the spraying castor oil as it is for any aerodynamic purpose; even so, the pilot usually emerges from a flight saturated in oil. The instrumentation is 'basic' — one engine speed indicator — and the controls are elementary. The engine is controlled by three levers: a throttle lever, of doubtful practicality, an air lever, and a fuel supply fine adjustment lever. There is a brass magneto switch and an engine cutout 'blip' button on the steering wheel for briefly cutting the engine for low power control.

The present engine is No 683, obtained from Ron Shelley of Billericay at about the same time as the original restoration was done, and had been fitted previously to the Sopwith SL.T.B.P., the progenitor of the Pup.

There are no ailerons, lateral control being achieved by wing warpings, controlled by turning the wheel. The tail section is reasonably conventional, with large elevators controlled by moving the wheel, which is mounted on a pivoted column, upwards to lower the elevators, and downwards to raise them, and a rudder operated by pedals which are too far away for comfort.

As with all the pre-1914 aircraft, flying is restricted to very still days or, more correctly, very still evenings, although of all of Shuttleworth's early types, excepting the replica Boxkite which has a modern 100hp engine, the Blackburn seems the toughest. Visitors who have tried to leave Old Warden early to avoid the rush will have missed seeing this aircraft climb slowly over the cornfield in the dim but atmospheric light from the setting sun.

The Shuttleworth Collection's Blackburn Type D Monoplane, registered BAPC-5, is the oldest airworthy British aircraft in the world, and, of course, it is completely unique.

Luftverkers-Gesellschaft (LVG) CVI

The Shuttleworth Collection's LVG C VI is the only airworthy, genuine World War I, German aircraft in Europe and the only other one known anywhere in the world is Cole Palen's refurbished Fokker D VII at Old Rhinebeck. This is not a reflection on the German aircraft industry, but a result of the conditions of the Treaty of Versailles which insisted that all aircraft belonging to the defeated central powers were to be destroyed. The Shuttleworth LVG C VI escaped this destruction because it was brought back to Britain for evaluation, having been shot down by SE5 As of No 74 Squadron, RAF, on 2 August 1918. The C VI was the last of the machines built by LVG to see service during World War I, and was used in large numbers in front line service. In the C-type two-seat armed reconnaissance aircraft category, it served a dual role, as a reconnaissance plane and light bomber.

Although not as well known as Fokkers and Albatrosses, the LVG C VI's antecedents made quite a name for themselves. The first bombs to be dropped on London were released from an LVG C II in November 1916, in broad daylight. The designer, Fritz Schneider, left the company after working on the little produced C IV to be replaced by Sabersky-Mussigbrod whose C V was a very popular aircraft used on reconnaissance, observation and light bombing duties. The C VI of 1917 was a redesigned C V; visibility was improved considerably by staggering the wings and making cutouts in the top wing. The fuselage was deepened and the armament improved. The fuselage was a boxlike construction of plywood over ribs and stringers while the wings were covered with lozenge pattern fabric.

Shuttleworth's LVG was built at Johannnistal bei Berlin in 1917. It was powered by a 230hp Benz engine, which gave excellent service on many German aircraft and, in common with the contemporary Mercedes engine its exhaust pipe rose high above the upper wing.

When the RAF acquired the aircraft, it was taken to Martlesham Heath, Suffolk, for evaluation. In August 1919 it was passed to the Imperial War Museum, London, which, lacking space, passed it on to the Science Museum, London, who had no space either, so the machine was never exhibited. In 1932 it returned to the Air Ministry and into store again, emerging briefly for the 1937 Hendon Show. In 1937 the machine was passed on yet again, but this time to the Shuttleworth Collection which did have space for it, and also the time and resources to restore it.

It took over five years to get it back into flying condition, as it had suffered quite a lot during its period of inactivity. The airframe was completely rebuilt, using as many original members as possible. A new fuel tank had to be made and modifications to the engine had to be incorporated so that engine-driven pumps from a Gipsy Queen could be used, because the original pumps were missing. The floats from the carburettor were also missing and new ones had to be made. It was found that the rudder was ineffective, so when a new one was needed it was made slightly oversize to improve the machine's handling.

The first flight was on 28 September 1972, piloted by Alan Wheeler. There were no pilot's notes to help, so the aircraft had to be treated like a prototype machine. The pilot's comment afterwards was that it handled like a big Tiger Moth! Since then, the aircraft has been a regular member of the Old Warden flight line, and is often to be seen flying in the company of a British contemporary machine.

Regular visitors to Old Warden will remember the day that, without warning, Geoff Wilderspin in the observer's seat, opened fire on Roger Hoefling, the commentator, and the crowd. The machine is normally equipped with a Parabellum on a movable mounting, but in this case a theatrical prop had been borrowed from the BBC who had been filming in the area.

In 1976 the LVG developed engine trouble while being flown by Neil Williams and, as a result, the landing was rather heavy, doing some damage to the undercarriage and the left lower wing. There had also been some worry about the wood drying out, which is always a problem with old aircraft. During the course of the repair work, a sample of the wood was sent to British Aerospace and tested, but was found to be within the allowed limits. The wings were re-covered and the Luftverkehrs-Gesellschaft C VI took to the air again in 1979.

Shuttleworth's immaculately restored LVG C VI is a very rare bird indeed, not only in itself but as a genuine airworthy World War I German aircraft.
Top: It has been restored with the distinctive five-colour lozenge pattern fabric typical of late-World War I German aircraft.
Right: The movable Parabellum machine gun for the observer is a faithful restoration. The armed C-Type reconnaissance aircraft replaced the un-armed, and vulnerable, B-Type reconnaissance aircraft from mid-1915. Note also the radiator above the upper wing centre-section.

Avro 504K

The Avro 504 was an improvement of the Avro 500, A V Roe's first successful aeroplane. Hinged ailerons replaced wing-warping. Powered originally by an 80hp Gnome rotary, it gained its circular engine cowlings only a month after its first flight at Brooklands in September 1913. The 504 was quickly adapted by the Royal Flying Corps and Royal Naval Air Service (who referred to it as the Avro 179). They were impressed by its speed of 81mph, rate of climb of 1000ft in 1 minute, 45 seconds, and its record-breaking ceiling of 14,420ft.

To an Avro 504 fell the unenviable honour of being the first British aeroplane lost in action, on 22 August 1914, but the score was evened on the 25th when a 504 piloted by Lt Wilson, with Lt Rabagliati as marksman, accounted for the first enemy machine. It was four Avro 504s of the RNAS which made the famous attack on the Friedrichshafen Zeppelin sheds on 21 November 1914, the first planned bombing raid.

Several variants followed: a single-seat Zeppelin fighter, an armed two-seater with a fixed fin and new rudder substituted for the familiar 'comma' balanced rudder, and a gunnery trainer with a machine gun fore and aft. In the Avro 504J, powered by a 100hp Gnome Monosoupape the aircraft assumed its most enduring role, for with this machine a syllabus of training was perfected which served the British flying services for many years. By the end of 1917 the 100hp Monosoupape was obsolete and the Avro 504K was developed with an engine mounting designed to accommodate any suitable power plant, such as the Clerget rotary or the inline, water-cooled Sunbeam Dyak.

The aeroplane owned by the Shuttleworth Collection is the only one of two surviving airworthy 504Ks in the world to be flown regularly, the other being G-CYCK at the National Aeronautical Collection, Rockcliffe, Ontario. The aircraft was found resting on the top of some shelving in the workshops of the old Airspeed Factory at Portsmouth. The engine had been removed and for some reason the fabric had been stripped off the airframe, which, luckily, was still in good condition. Brian Lewis, who found the aircraft in 1951, started to restore it in a corner of the workshop. Two years later Lewis joined the RAF and the 504 was removed to a hut owned by his father. No further work was done on it and eventually it was acquired by a film company to be used in making *Reach for the Sky*.

The re-build for the film was finished by Avro apprentices at Woodford and after the film the aircraft was presented to the Shuttleworth Collection. The original engine, an Armstrong-Siddeley Lynx, had been left in Lewis' shed, so in order to get the 504 in the air for the film a 110hp Le Rhône engine which had been in a Hanriot biplane, acquired by Richard Shuttleworth before World War II, was fitted. The Avro 504K was grounded from July 1972 to October 1976 and during that time a new engine was obtained from Frank Tallman in America, which, after stripping and re-building by Wally Berry, was fitted to the re-fabricated airframe.

The early history of the machine is not so clear. It had definitely been converted for glider towing because the fuselage was strengthened and Lewis removed the winch gear in 1952, but that is where the history ends. Based on interviews which Mr Lewis conducted with ex-Airspeed employees it was thought that the serial number when it first came to Airspeed was BK892 which had been painted over a civil registration. However, this information was based upon a person remembering the aircraft being at Airspeed in 1939. The history of BK892 can be traced: previously, it had been G-ADEV and originally H5199, and had certainly been converted for glider towing, but according to RAF records it had gone as instructional airframe 3118M to No 1264 Squadron, Air Training Corps, at Windermere in 1942. This was confirmed by the then Signals Officer of the ATC, who later became the CO, Bill Aspinwall, who not only remembers the aircraft arriving, but oversaw its departure in December 1946 when a low-loader from Catterick came and took it away doing rather a lot of damage in the process. This means that it is very unlikely that the aircraft found at Airspeed was BK892: indeed, according to the RAF records, instructional airframe 3118M is still in the service. This certainly highlights the problem of identifying some of these old aircraft. Records going back that far are quite rare, memories are not infallible, and despite much research by several people independently no clear-cut, confirmable story emerges.

Top: A piece of vintage atmosphere at Old Warden as the Shuttleworth Collection's Avro 504K is started by their Huck's Starter. This is a Ford Model T chassis with a shaft, driven via gears from the engine crankshaft, which is inserted into the propeller boss: the car's engine is revved, thus turning the aircraft's engine, saving the hand-swinging process.
Right: The 504 is very stable in flight.

Royal Aircraft Factory SE5A G-EBIA

The SE5 was designed by H P Folland at the Royal Aircraft Factory, Farnborough, Hampshire, in 1916. Powered by a liquid-cooled 150hp Hispano-Suiza 8A engine, with a car-type radiator, the airframe was of conventional wire-braced, spruce construction, and covered with fabric. The cockpit was almost entirely enclosed, a luxury instantly abandoned at the Front, where the SE5 arrived in April 1917, with the élite No 56 Squadron, with Albert Ball among its pilots. Inherent stability had been a design requirement, for the benefit of the often inexperienced young pilots, and this made it less manoeuvrable than the nervous Sopwith Camel, which, however, had a reputation for spinning. An excellent gun platform, the SE5 was armed with a 0.303in Vickers machine gun offset to port on the cowling, firing through the propeller arc by means of Constantinesco synchronising gear. The top centre section carried a 0.303in Lewis machine gun on a Foster mounting, down which the gun could be pulled to facilitate magazine changing, or upward firing, recognition of Ball's successes in a similarly armed Nieuport Nie 17.

By June 1917 the SE5A was replacing the SE5. It was powered by a 200hp Hispano-Suiza and retained the shorter span wings introduced on the second batch of SE5s. Problems with the reduction gear and shortage of the French engine, led to re-engining the SE5A with the ungeared (direct drive) 200hp Wolseley W.4A Viper based on the 200hp Hispano-Suiza. However, a variety of Hispano-Suiza engines were used to ease production and supply. The SE5A was strong, well armed, had excellent flying characteristics, was faster than German fighters and, until the advent of the Fokker D VII in April 1918, was unmatched in performance at high altitude.

SE5A serial number F904 was built at Wolseley Motors' Addersley Park factory, Birmingham, with constructor's number 645, and reached its squadron during the last months of World War I. When the war ended it was declared surplus, and having had little use it was sold off for civilian use. In 1924 it joined Major J C Savage's famous Skywriting Company at Hendon as G–EBIA. Here it was probably modified to include a tank within the fuselage to contain the chemicals which would produce smoke when fed into specially lengthened exhaust pipes, which met in a 'Y' junction at the stern post. Withdrawn from use in February 1928, at some time it left Hendon and wound up suspended, engineless, from the rafters in the flight shed of Armstrong Whitworth at Baginton, Coventry. In 1955 Air Commodore Alan Wheeler discovered it, and secured it for the Shuttleworth Collection.

Unfortunately the restoration was beyond the capacity of the Collection, but a formal agreement with the Royal Aircraft Establishment, successor to the Royal Aircraft Factory, Farnborough, was made. In return for effective joint ownership, supplying pilots and the right to display the aeroplane at RAE functions, the work would be done at Farnborough. Virtually all woodwork was re-made and missing metal fittings made up from scratch. The absence of comprehensive drawings meant the use of rotten parts as patterns, and the use of informed guesswork where nothing survived at all. Three engines were found; a low-compression 150hp Hispano-Suiza from the USA was swapped for a 200hp Viper and radiator found in an Essex garage owner's collection, but it was the London Science Museum's 200hp Hispano-Suiza which was installed. At some time an engine had been captured by the Germans, who had made meticulous notes from which, forty years later, the RAE worked while refurbishing their engine. By an amazing twist of fate the serial number quoted in the notes matched the Science Museum's specimen! A brand-new propeller was bought from an RAF officer at Lyneham. Although many of the team were old hands, many skills had to be re-learned, particularly airframe rigging, and they were constantly impressed by the quality and intricacy of the wood- and metal-work required. The aeroplane was positively identified when a pencil note of its original civil registration was found on some of old fabric — G–EBIA.

On 4 August 1959, two years and four months after work had commenced, Air Commodore Alan Wheeler test flew the SE5A after a brief taxi run. The aeroplane flew regularly at Shuttleworth displays until 26 July 1972, when it was damaged after a forced landing, following a crankshaft failure. However, the structural repairs proved less of a headache for the RAE than reconditioning the spare Viper, the Hispano-Suiza having been too badly damaged to be repaired, and it was four years before the SE5A again took to the air, in the hands of Wing Commander David Bywater, on 16 December 1976.

SE5A F904 was restored for the Shuttleworth Trust by RAE Farnborough, where it is hangared for part of the year. It appears regularly at Shuttleworth air displays, and at the bi-annual SBAC Farnborough International public air displays. It now flies in 'factory-fresh' finish without squadron markings due to doubts about their authenticity.

Bristol F2B Fighter G-AEPH

Captain Frank Barnwell of the British and Colonial Aeroplane Company (Bristol) was responsible for several of the most interesting aeroplane designs of World War I. These included the Bristol Scout of 1915; it was while flying one of these, No 1611, that Captain Lanoe Hawker of No 6 Squadron, RFC, armed only with a single-shot carbine, drove down one, damaged a second and shot down in flames a third enemy aircraft on 25 July 1915. All three were armed with machine guns and Hawker was awarded the first Victoria Cross for aerial combat. Another Barnwell design was the Bristol M1 monoplane, of 1911–17, the potential of which was never seriously exploited because of official pro-biplane prejudice.

In early 1916 Barnwell started work on a two-seat reconnaissance aircraft, the R2A, which was soon redesigned completely to suit the new 150hp Rolls-Royce Falcon V-type engine, and redesignated the F2A. Although the aeroplane was armed with a forward-firing Vickers 0.303in machine gun under the cowling, and used Constantinesco synchronising gear, this was at first seen only as a supplement to the conventionally-sited 0.303in Lewis machine gun mounted on a flexible Scarff ring in the observer's cockpit. Nor, at this time, was the strength and manoeuvrability of the aeroplane realised. On its operational début in April 1917 with No 48 Squadron, RFC, it was flown like a two-seat aircraft, and four out of six were shot down by five Albatros D IIIs led by Manfred von Richthofen. However, a few pilots began to use the F2A's armament offensively, concentrating on the Vickers, and using the Lewis for rear defence, reversing the priority of the weapon and turning the tables.

Modified as the F2B, by continuing and covering the lower wing aerofoil section through the centre section, improving forward visibility by sloping the longerons from the observer's cockpit to the level of the engine bearer, and chord and span adjustments to the tail surfaces, the Bristol F2B Fighter or 'Brisfit' displayed a potency which eventually made it the most versatile fighting machine of the war. Various engines were used, no fewer than seventeen, usually because of the heavy demand for Rolls-Royce units, but the most successful was the 275hp Rolls-Royce Falcon III V-12 first installed in 1917. The flexible power delivery, smoothness — and cleanness — of the Falcon, particularly, was a revelation to pilots accustomed to coping with the idiosyncrasies of rotary engines. The F2B equipped fourteen full RAF squadrons by the Armistice of November 1918, at which time 3001 had been accepted.

After World War I the F2B continued in service for fourteen years, adding light bombing and army co-operation to its wartime offensive patrol, high-speed reconnaissance and fighter roles. It remained in production until 1926. No 6 Squadron was the last RAF squadron to retire its F2Bs, in Iraq in 1932. The type also served in Egypt, Germany, India, and Turkey. It was exported to several countries, and licence built in Belgium, the USA, and Sweden.

Although first flown at Filton, Bristol, in June 1918, the Bristol F2B Fighter D8096 did not see wartime action, but was converted soon after the war to Mark II configuration which suited it to its army co-operation role during troubled times in Turkey, where it is believed to have served with No 208 Squadron. In the mid-1920s a further conversion to Mark III standard dual-control followed. Earmarked for civil conversion in 1936, the aircraft was purchased by the veteran aircraft collector C P B Ogilvie, and although allotted the civil registration G–AEPH it had still not been converted when, after years of storage in a shed at Elstree Aerodrome, it was acquired by the Shuttleworth Collection. With it was a spare engine and other parts and a Huck's Starter, which is now used at Old Warden. Restoration had started when, in 1950, Bristol asked if their company could do the work in order to fly the F2B when King George VI visited the giant Brabazon airliner. On Saint Valentine's day, 1951, the restored veteran flew again, piloted by A J (Bill) Pegg, Chief Test Pilot of the Bristol Aeroplane Company. It was complete with Scarff gun ring and its original serial number. The Falcon III of D8096 is now the oldest Rolls-Royce aero-engine still operating, and it is ironic that the Bristol fighter has already outlived the Brabazon by over twenty-five years, continuing to fly regularly at Shuttleworth Collection flying days.

The Shuttleworth Trust Collection's Bristol F2B Fighter, D8096, is the only airworthy F2B in the world, and its Falcon III is the oldest Rolls-Royce aero-engine still operating. After the 1980 air display season the aircraft was dismantled for a thorough overhaul restoration, and repainting in appropriate World War I drab.

Sopwith Pup G-EBKY

It is said that the original design of the SL.T.B.P. 'Runabout', Sopwith Chief Test Pilot Harry Hawker's personal aeroplane of 1915, was sketched out in chalk on Sopwith's experimental shop floor. It was a derivative of the pre-World War I Tabloid racer and, with its simple structure and 50hp Gnome engine, prefigured many of the qualities of the agile scouts to come. From this machine, Herbert Smith developed a design for a single-seat scout, with an 80hp rotary engine. The drawings were passed early in 1916, and by 12 April Hawker had set a new British altitude record of 24,408ft in the new aeroplane. Sopwiths were unable to cope with producing the numbers ordered first by the RNAS and then by the RFC as they were already heavily committed to the manufacture of 1½-Strutters and Triplanes, so the Standard Motor Company, Whitehead Aircraft Company and William Beardmore Company Limited were appointed as sub-contractors.

The RNAS tested the single-seat scout at Furnes in France in May 1916. Produced to standards agreed between the Admiralty and Sopwiths, the aeroplane was officially designated the Type 9901, but despite strict orders, became known affectionately as the Pup.

In Autumn 1916 the first Pups arrived in France, going to 'B' Flight of No 8 (Naval) Squadron, No 1 Wing, RNAS; by December 'Naval Eight' was the first all-Pup-equipped squadron in action. The first RFC Pup unit reached the Front on 24 December. At this time RNAS men and machines were flying under RFC command and a period of co-operation began which laid the foundations of the RAF.

The Pup was universally praised for its flying characteristics, for not only could it turn inside any opponent but, with a ceiling of 18,000ft, had the height advantage. For the first time the British pilots felt their machines gave them an edge. But the Pup was not without problems. The canvas ammunition belts of the single 0.303in Vickers machine gun, which fired through the propeller arc by means of the Sopwith-Kauper synchronisation-gear, froze and its lubricating oils stiffened at maximum service ceiling, causing malfunctions. The Le Rhône 9C engine gave trouble and the aeroplane was so light that a strong wind could easily overturn it on the ground. Nevertheless it was a potent fighting machine. 'Naval Eight's' victory score for the eight flyable days of December 1916 was thirteen enemy aircraft to its Pups, plus three to its Nieuports. A year later, November and December 1917 provided twenty victories. The Pup served RNAS and RFC squadrons in France until early 1918, and also with Home Defence squadrons. On 2 August 1918 a Pup flown by Squadron Commander E H Dunning was the first aircraft to land on a moving aircraft carrier.

After the war a few Pups were civilianised and Sopwith produced ten purpose-built two-seaters and called them Doves. The first public appearance of the Dove was in May 1919, at Hounslow, and such was the display mounted by its pilot, that the Prince of Wales (the late Duke of Windsor) enthusiastically requested a flight. Accordingly T O M Sopwith accorded him the honour of an exhilarating ride in the rear cockpit, behind Major W G Barker, VC. But the King was not at all enamoured by the thought that the heir to the throne had been at the mercy not only of a prototype, but also of a convalescent pilot, still with an arm in a sling as a result of a combat in which he was wounded three times, yet accounted for four enemy aircraft! He banned his son flying for many years!

Sopwith Dove G-EKBY was first registered in 1925 to D L Hollis Williams, but was built between 1919 and 1920. In September 1920 Sopwith Aviation was wound up. Its successor, H G Hawker Engineering Co Ltd was formed next month, but this Dove did not re-appear for several years, becoming the property of Williams on 27 March 1925. It seems that in early 1927 his employers, Fairey Aviation, performed a major overhaul on it, the parts required, with several spares, supplied by Hawker. However, the greatest change was the fitting of a metal Sopwith Snipe tail fin and horn-balanced rudder.

In September 1930 title passed to the Dove's co-owner, C H Lowe-Wylde, designer and Managing Director of the British Aircraft Company, Maidstone Airport (West Malling), Kent. There on 13 May 1933 he was killed whilst demonstrating his BAC Planette No 1 motorised glider, when he became ill in flight.

Abandoned at West Malling, the Dove was eventually purchased by Richard Shuttleworth who, with drawings supplied by Hawker, converted it to Pup configuration. In 1937–38 the wings lost their sweep, and, with the tailplane, assumed the scout's raked tips. The rudder lost its horn balance to look authentic and the aircraft became a single-seater. Flown as a Pup on 26 February 1938, bearing spurious serial N5184, it now flies as N5180, the first naval production Pup, a Naval Eight machine.

Shuttleworth's Pup is regularly flown by John Lewis, Rolls-Royce's Chief Test Pilot.

de Havilland DH51 G-EBIR

Just before World War I aviation was still very much in its infancy. The publicity in Britain and Europe resulting from the cross-Channel flight made the public aware that aircraft were no longer a curiosity, but a viable proposition. Schools were started to instruct would-be pilots in the rudimentary skills, but the aircraft then available were still quite primitive. Competitions and air races started to improve the standard of machine, but had hardly produced results by the time World War I had started. Although slow at first to take to the aeroplane, military thinking eventually did start to embrace aviation and with the concentration of manpower and resources that only war can bring, the development of aircraft over the four years of hostilities was so rapid that the aircraft in 1918 bore little resemblance to those of 1914.

Many ex-RAF aircraft were released onto the civilian market to be used in flying clubs, for aerial publicity such as banner towing and sky writing, postal services and airlines. These sufficed for a year or so and then gradually new designs started to appear. De Havilland's were in the forefront, first with airliners like the DH18 and DH34 and, later, along with the building of 'one- or two-offs' for specific purposes, such as the King's Cup Race, they started to aim deliberately for the potentially large market of private and club aircraft. The DH50, built in 1923, proved itself to be a very fine aircraft and, although only seventeen were made, they gained many honours and set high standards for others to follow. In 1923 the next aircraft to be rolled out at de Havilland's factory at Stag Lane, Edgware, Middlesex, was the small low-wing monoplane, the DH53, which became known as the Humming Bird. At the other end of the market was the large three-seat touring biplane, the DH51, which first flew a year later in 1924.

Originally designed for the war surplus 90hp Royal Aircraft Factory 1a engine, it had typical de Havilland construction of plywood over spruce longerons and cross-struts, and fabric-covered wings with streamlined wire bracing. The registration authorities were not happy with this engine and so a war-surplus 120hp Airdisco V-S engine was fitted. The Aircraft Disposal Corporation had re-built the heavy Renault V-8 power plant, fitting, amongst other things, an aluminium cylinder head and, in fact, managed to increase the power to 140hp. Only three DH51s were built: the first two lasted less than eight years, but it is the third one, built in 1925, which is still flying.

The DH51 was not quite the right aircraft for the private market and in 1925 de Havilland produced their first 'Moth', the DH60, which showed so much potential that Sir Sefton Brancker, the Director of Civil Aviation, recommended the formation of government-subsidised flying clubs to be equipped with Moths.

DH51 G-EBIR was registered to J E Carberry some three months after the flight of the first DH60 Moth, and it was shipped out to Mombasa in Kenya and taken by road to Nyeri, at the foot of Mount Kenya, finishing the journey by ox-cart. The longest flight it undertook while over there was a three hundred and thirty mile round trip to collect Sir Sefton Brancker from Kisumu.

G-EBIR was re-registered in Kenya, first as G-KAA and then, when Kenya was allotted its own prefix, it became the first aircraft on the Kenyan register as VP-KAA. In 1928 it was transferred to Tom Campbell-Black (who later flew the DH88 Comet Racer *Grosvenor House*), G Skinner and A Hughes, and in 1933 G Onslow became the new owner. During World War II VP-KAA, or *Miss Kenya* as she was called, was stored at Eastleigh, Kenya, but flew again afterwards in the hands of G Baudet. Following some damage inflicted in 1951, Le Poer Trench restored *Miss Kenya* back to flying condition. She was later owned by Messrs Johnstone and Wilson.

In 1965 the aircraft was flown in a Blackburn Beverley back to Britain where de Havilland, now Hawker Siddeley, refurbished her and got her back into flying condition before presenting her, as G-EBIR again, to the Shuttleworth Collection.

Despite the 140hp engine driving the impressive four-blade wooden propeller, *Miss Kenya* is quite a docile machine to fly. In fact when she was first flown in Britain, she felt 'as if her ailerons were set in concrete'. Later, a routine inspection revealed that she should have had differential ailerons and when the re-conversion was made G-EBIR once again became a well-mannered and vice-free machine.

Right: *Shuttleworth's elegant DH51 is the third and last built and the only one to survive.*

Top: *More than one man is required to turn the DH51's engine due to its high compression. The second man is also necessary to pull the first clear of the propellor because the four blades follow each other rather rapidly! Originally, it could be started using a magneto handle in the cockpit together with an external one, similar to pre-war military aircraft*

Hawker Tomtit G-AFTA

In the late 1920s, Hawker's brilliant designer Sydney Camm (who later designed the Hurricane) was responsible for their answer to the RAF's requirement for a basic trainer to replace the venerable Avro 540N, the Tomtit, an equispan, single-bay, tandem two-seat biplane. The Air Ministry specified the five-cylinder, air-cooled, 150hp Armstrong-Siddeley Mongoose radial engine, which would be more economical to operate than the 240hp Lynx of the Avro. However, various engines were installed, including the Cirrus Hermes and the Wolseley AR9.

In respect not only of the intention to phase out the RAF's wood and wire tradesmen, but also in conformity with the new generation of metal-structure combat machines, the Tomtit utilised the all-metal construction techniques also used in Camm's superlative Fury fighter and Hart day bomber. Developed at the same time as these, it shared their steel and duralumin tubular space frame fuselage, and the simple, weight-reducing innovation of pinch-formed 'flats' at the ends of vertical and horizontal members for attachment. A further advantage was the standardisation of basic structural materials, which could be applied over a range of different types of airframe. The Tomtit also gained some of the Fury's sleekness.

The Tomtit also featured more sophisticated control surfaces and instruments. Frise ailerons were fitted to the lower wings only, to counteract the yaw often induced in a turn, and Handley-Page slots were fitted to the leading-edge of the upper wings to give much better control at high angles of attack. The student pilot's cockpit could be hooded over for blind flying practice, for which the Reid and Sigrist instrument panel, featuring the new Reid turn and bank indicator, was provided. Well-staggered wings were designed specifically to assist evacuation by parachute from both cockpits.

When first flown by Hawker's test pilot P W S 'George' Bulman. at Brooklands, Surrey, in November 1928, the Tomtit turned out to be a delightfully aerobatic aeroplane. It could perform all the evolutions of the more powerful fighters of its day. At its military trials at Martlesham Heath, Suffolk, the RAF were enthusiastic and within three months an order for ten machines had been placed. Unhappily the effects of the Depression ultimately restricted the total RAF commitment to only twenty-five aeroplanes. The cheaper and simpler DH82 Tiger Moth was ordered in quantity instead.

The Tomtit was displayed at the 1929 Olympia Aero Show alongside Camm's other new designs, the Hawker Hart and Fury. Serving with the RAF between 1929 and 1931, the Tomtit equipped No 3 Flying Training School, the Central Flying School, Upavon, Wiltshire, and also No 24 Squadron, and several Group flights, on communication duties. The Tomtit was adopted as a standard basic trainer by the Royal Canadian Air Force.

K1786 was the last Hawker Tomtit to be built for the RAF in 1930. It served with No 3 Flying Training School at Grantham, Lincolnshire, and with Nos 23 and 5 Group Communications Flights from 1932, when the Avro Tutor took over its training role. In 1935 the aircraft became obsolete and K1786 was 'civilianised' by C B Field, Kingswood Knoll, Surrey, to be passed on as G-AFTA to the Leicestershire Aero Club which, by 1939, was operating four Tomtits. During the war Alex Henshaw, Chief Pilot for Vickers Armstrong's Castle Bromwich factory, needing supplementary aircraft for communications, bought three of these. The Tomtit was always capable of landing on a sixpence, and he would often use the field alongside his house at Hampton in Arden, when long hours testing Spitfires made him late for dinner. At this time G-AFTA acquired a streamlined headrest and a Spitfire windscreen for the rear cockpit.

In 1946 the Tomtit went to G P Shea-Simmons and later that year to G Goodhew at Kidlington, Oxfordshire, to be bought by R C S Stafford-Allen at Chalgrove in 1947 to serve as a glider-tug. For just over a year, before Hawker purchased it in July 1950, their Chief Test Pilot, Neville Duke, displayed the Tomtit's aerobatic racing form. It then flew with their Hart and Hurricane, immaculate in Hawker's royal blue and gold lining until it was passed on to the Shuttleworth Collection and re-finished as the original K1786. Since the 1950s, G-AFTA has been the sole, known remaining, and certainly the only airworthy Tomtit.

Top: *Ground crew hold down the tail of Shuttleworth's Hawker Tomtit Mk I, G-AFTA, as the pilot performs pre-flight power checks before an air display at Old Warden.*
Right: *Since the grounding some years ago of the RAF's Hawker Hart, J9941, now in the RAF Museum at Hendon, the Tomtit has been the sole representative of Hawker's pre-war aircraft, but it is soon to be joined by Shuttleworth's Afghan Hind.*

Comper CLA.7 Swift G-AT G-ACTF

Nicholas Comper joined the RFC in 1915, having worked under Geoffrey de Havilland as a technical apprentice of the Aircraft Manufacturing Company. After seeing action during the war, he spent a year at Cambridge University reading aerodynamics, before serving at Upavon, Farnborough and Cranwell. At RAF College, Cranwell, he and a group of fellow lecturers and students formed the Cranwell Light Aeroplane Club, and he headed a design team which built four aeroplanes. In 1929, he resigned his RAF commission and went into business. The first Comper aircraft, the CLA.7, flew that December and had clearly evolved from one of his Cranwell designs, the CLA.3. It was named Swift. It was produced with several different engines, but by 1931 the Pobjoy 'R', seven-cylinder, geared radial had become standard. Douglas Pobjoy had served with Comper at Cranwell, where he had designed the original 'P' engine, and in 1931 opened his own factory close by Comper's at Hooten Park aerodrome. The remarkable 'R' engine developed 75 brake horsepower, but weighed only 135lbs dry, giving the Comper CLA.7 Swift a rate of climb of 140ft/min, a cruising speed of 120mph and top speed of 140mph, which was close to the performance of contemporary RAF fighters. The single-seat Swift was of all-wood construction, and was fabric-covered, except for plywood rear decking. It had folding wings, requiring no jury struts, or the disconnection of aileron controls.

The French Motor Car Company of Bombay, Calcutta and Delhi were Comper's Indian agents. In 1932 they ordered two Swifts, one being VT–ADO on behalf of Alban Ali, a tea planter from Silchar, Assam, who had learned to fly in England, with the Newcastle Aero Club. His enthusiasm for the Swift stemmed from what he had read in the aviation press. His was the ninth of the 1932 batch, test flown by Nick Comper on 24 August before crating and despatch. On arrival in India VT–ADO was re-erected and rigged at the Bengal Flying Club, and tested by the Chief Flying Instructor, W Dougal. Two days later, on 10 October, Alban Ali flew his new aeroplane for the first time, which performed 'like a galvanometer'! After a couple of days of familiarisation he flew home through the monsoon rain to Silchar. From a nearby polo ground he flew many hours cross-country for the next three months, often on business.

In 1933 he planned to fly to England, timing his arrival in Delhi to coincide with the Viceroy's Challenge Trophy race in which he intended to fly.

Also competing were Richard Shuttleworth in Swift G–ABPY, and his friend George Stead in the Gipsy II-powered Swift, G–ACBY, who had both flown in from Old Warden, Bedfordshire. None of the Swifts won, but Stead made the fastest time, 153mph, and Ali the second fastest, completing the 699 miles at 124.3mph. Shuttleworth had to force land in a village street. At the end of February 1933, Ali and Stead departed for England intending to cross Persia, Iraq, Palestine and Egypt. All went well until they flew into a sandstorm near Ur which later caused them considerable trouble, for in Iraq and Palestine Ali's 'Scarlet Angel' had to force land several times in the desert and needed running repairs. Finally at Abu Sueir in Egypt another forced landing wrecked the undercarriage and propeller. After two week's work Ali flew on to Cairo and there left his aeroplane.

Bought by George Errington, a Comper engineer and inspector, VT–ADO arrived at the new plant at Heston and was restored to airworthiness a year later, registered G–ACTF. Errington became Airspeed's test pilot and flew the Swift until the outbreak of war in 1939, from Southampton. Impressed into the RAF the aeroplane acquired a windscreen, parachute seat and armour-plated fuel piping in 1942.

G–ACTF re-surfaced in 1949 being prepared by Airspeed test pilot Ron Clear for the Daily Express race the next year. Special fairing, a streamlined hood and high-speed undercarriage spats helped her set up an FAI class record at 141mph, flying into fifth place.

'Scarlet Angel' changed hands at least twice more during the next thirty years, in 1955 to J Quinney of Sambourn, and in 1965 to Bill Woodhams, who overhauled it. She was certified as airworthy again in 1969. Her present owner, Alan Chalkley, bought her in January 1973 and after a scrupulous re-build by Joe Austin of Personal Planes Services, she is now flying out of Wycombe Air Park with the Pobjoy Niagara engine installed by her previous owner.

Right: G–ACTF is one of four airworthy Comper CLA.7 Swifts currently on the British Civil Register, the others being G–ABTC, G–ABUS and G–ABUU. G–ACTF has had a very active career, in the hands of several owners, spanning five decades.
Top: Starting Swift G–ACTF using the time-honoured method of pushing a petrol-soaked rag into the carburettor intake.

Percival Mew Gull G-AEXF

One of three similar aeroplanes, derived from the E.1 racer of 1934, designed specifically as racers by Edgar W Percival, this Mew Gull was built in 1936 for the Schlesinger Race to Johannesburg. Of all-wood construction, ZS–AHM was powered by a Gipsy Six Series II engine fitted with a constant speed propeller, and had split flaps hinged to the rear spar which provided lift and drag at low speeds. Named *The Golden City* for the race, and flown by the South African pioneer aviator, Major Alastair Miller, it retired at Belgrade after fuel problems forced a landing. Re-registered to Alex Henshaw in 1937 as G–AEXF, it was re-fitted with a standard Gipsy Six and raced all that year, often against Edgar Percival and Charles Gardner in their Mew Gulls, and won the Folkestone Trophy at 210mph. The Mew Gull was, in fact, faster than contemporary biplane fighters and, despite a difference of 840hp, was only 16mph slower than the first production Supermarine Spitfire Mk Is! In the winter of 1937–38 Henshaw and Jack Cross of Essex Aero Ltd installed a Gipsy Six 'R' engine and a Ratier variable pitch airscrew from the DH88 Comet racer G–ACSS.

Henshaw and Giles Guthrie clashed in the Isle of Man Races. Then, at the King's Cup they met Edgar Percival. Henshaw's Mew Gull now had a longer nose, flat-topped cowling and a de Havilland constant speed propeller with a conical spinner. The rear decking was modified to suit a lower canopy; the pilot sat virtually on the floor. At 236.25mph it beat Guthrie into second place and Percival came sixth. Having won the premier British air race, the King's Cup, at a speed never bettered by a British aircraft, the Mew Gull returned to Essex Aero Ltd over winter, to be readied for its second Cape record attempt. Long-range fuel tanks and radio were installed, and a Gipsy Six Series II was fitted again.

Between 5 and 9 February 1939, Alex Henshaw completed the round trip from Portsmouth to Johannesburg and back in 4 days, 10 hours and 16 minutes, using rudimentary desert and jungle landing stages, taking the record from the DH88 Comet G–ACSS, set by Flying Officer A E Clouson and Betty Kirby Green in 1937; it still stands as an FAI Class Record. In July 1939 G–AEXF was sold to Victor Vermorel in France, but remained on the British register. Throughout the German occupation it was concealed, in pieces, it is said, under potato sacks near Villefranche-sur-Saône. Despite finding the log books the Germans never found the aeroplane. Vermorel was killed in a flying accident in 1945 and Jean Drapier bought the aircraft and began to

restore it at Lyon-Bron in 1947. Three years later Hugh Scrope approached Doug Bianchi (who later founded Personal Planes Services, specialising in maintaining vintage machines) with the idea of helping him retrieve the historic Mew Gull. He bought it for a reported one million francs and Bianchi and Ted Squires flew over to check the aircraft. Eventually Scrope flew it home.

After an 'argument with a ditch' at Shoreham, Doug Bianchi rebuilt the Mew Gull, enlarging the cockpit canopy for its new owner, J N Somers, who subsequently raced it. In 1955, with an even higher canopy, installed by Adie Aviation Ltd, Croydon, Peter Clifford, on behalf of the owner Fred Dunkerley, raced the Mew Gull to win the King's Cup for the second time at 213.5mph.

G–AEXF re-appeared from storage in 1962 to be raced with a Proctor's Gipsy Queen 2 engine, by J E G Appleyard. By 1965 there was yet another canopy, and a Proctor undercarriage installed. Finally, in the hands of E Crabtree, the engine blew up in practice for the National Air Races, and it suffered a forced landing at Catterick, Yorkshire. The Mew Gull became a museum piece, and was gradually mutilated by 'preservation' groups, until eventually bought by Tom Storey and Martin Barraclough of the Tiger Club for £175 each in 1972.

Storey and Barraclough restored the Mew Gull to as near as possible its original configuration, before its first modifications at Essex Aero in 1937, an enormous task. The wings had been sawn through outboard of the undercarriage, the elevator sawn in two, an aileron was missing, there was no engine or cowlings, and the woodwork was damp-and oil-damaged. Drawings were worked up with the help of Brian Mann and Roy West, and the major missing parts began to trickle in from enthusiasts' collections. The wings were re-built from scratch, with the help of Tom Smith and Alan Savior of Speedwell Sailplanes. In spring 1978 the irrepressible G–AEXF flew again at Redhill, Surrey, and made its public début on 25 June at Old Warden, flown by Brian Smith.

Top: *Brian Smith, reluctant to leave the cockpit of G–AEXF, the sole remaining Mew Gull.*
Right: *Percival Mew Gull G–AEXF still holds the FAI class record for the England to the Cape and return flight, for Alex Henshaw's 1939 flight from Portsmouth to Johannesburg and back.*

Gloster Gladiator MkI G-AMRK

Designed by Harry Folland's team as a private venture based on the Gloster Gauntlet, the prototype Gloster Gladiator first flew in April 1935 and the first production Gladiators entered service in January 1937. The Mark I had an 840hp Bristol Mercury IX nine-cylinder radial engine, compared with the 645hp of the Gauntlet, and the aerodynamics were much more sophisticated than those of the Gauntlet. The wings were single bay (i.e. one set of struts on each side) instead of two-bay structure, and both upper and lower wings had hydraulically operated flaps. The Dowty cantilever undercarriage with its simple external structure, the canopy, and combined Townend and exhaust collector ring reduced drag. Armament was four machine guns, two firing through the propeller and two fixed outboard under the lower wings.

In a way the Gladiator was obsolete by the time that hostilities had begun, but it proved itself to be a force to reckon with. The two most famous episodes in the Gladiator's career centre around the Sea Gladiator, during its service in Norway, operating from HMS *Glorious,* and the famous *Faith, Hope* and *Charity,* which were reputed to have defended Malta alone for several weeks in 1941. It appears that there were six assembled (and six crated) Sea Gladiators on Malta in June 1940, these would fly three at a time in rotation. But the Maltese, or rather the media, only seeing three of them at a time, gave them the now-famous names; Air Marshal Forster Maynard, AFC, the senior RAF officer on Malta in 1941, first heard the legend when he returned to Great Britain! There were also Hawker Hurricanes on the island during this period.

The Shuttleworth Gladiator is the only surviving flying Gladiator of the 747 built between 1934 and 1939. Nominally a Mark I, it is a composite aircraft made of parts from at least three machines. It flies with the markings of No 72 Squadron, RAF, as L8032, the original number of its present fuselage, made by Glosters at Brockwork in 1938.

Final assembly of the original airframe and fitting of the engine was done at No 27 Maintenance Unit, Shawbury, where it remained until 1941, when it joined No 2 Anti-Aircraft Co-operation Unit at Gosport. For a few months in 1943 it joined No 1624 Flight and then, apart from a few months with No 61 Operational Training Unit, and a visit to Marshalls of Cambridge for some repairs, it spent the rest of its military life in various MUs, until it was sold back to Glosters in 1948.

In 1950 it went as an instructional airframe to the Air Service Training establishment at Hamble and in 1951 it was joined there by another Gladiator, a Mark II, N5903, which had originally been built for the Iraqi Air Force in 1939, but had ended up at another Air Service Training establishment before joining L8032 at Hamble. Hamble was closed soon after and in December 1951 the two machines were bought for £5 each by Vivian L Bellamy of Flightways at Eastleigh, Hampshire. He used parts from N5903 to complete L8032 and registered the once again airworthy machine as G-AMRK, first flying one June evening in 1952. It was too costly to keep flying and in 1953 it was sold back to Glosters for £300, on condition it would remain airworthy. In 1957 a complete re-build was started with the encouragement of Gloster's Chief Test Pilot, Wing Commander R F Martin, OBE, DFC, and afterwards it was painted in the pre-war colours of No 72 Squadron, RAF, and mistakenly serialled K8032.

It was handed over to the Shuttleworth Trust in November 1960 and in the hands of Dicky Martin or John Lewis has proved to be one of the most exciting and reliable of the Collection's aircraft. After ten years of display work it was flown to Staverton, Gloucestershire, for a complete overhaul and re-covering by Flight One, and it was here that it was discovered that the port upper mainplane was from a third aircraft, a Sea Gladiator, probably fitted when it was with the Anti-Aircraft Co-operation Unit at Gosport in 1942. It was known to have had an accident at that time, and to have been repaired on site.

At last its correct serial number of L8032 was painted on, and it returned to Old Warden in June 1974. The exhaust collector ring began to show signs of wear during 1979 and a search was started for a new one. Although the full plans were available to make a new one, no jigs remained in existence so this option would have been too costly. The old collector ring was removed and repaired, but in the meantime a replacement from a Bristol Bolingbroke was found in Canada. This was fitted and once again the roar of the Mercury engine is to be heard across the quiet fields of Bedfordshire.

The last remaining airworthy Gloster Gladiator serialled L8032, owned by the Shuttleworth Trust, is built from the components of several machines. The fuselage mid-section is the part of an aircraft which identifies it, no matter what other parts are changed. It is often impossible to identify a restored aircraft.

Boeing Stearman A75N1 Kaydet G-AROY

In 1933, as part of a private venture, the Stearman Aircraft Company designed a tandem-seat primary Trainer, the Stearman Model 70, followed in 1934 by the Model A75. It became to America what the de Havilland DH82 Tiger Moth was to Britain: developed as a series, more were produced than any other biplane.

Floyd Stearman established Stearman Aircraft Inc in 1926, and produced a series of successful mailplanes. In 1929 the company became part of the United Aircraft Corporation, Floyd Stearman left the company shortly afterwards. In 1934 Stearman became a subsidiary of Boeing. It is ironical that the company's best known and most successful design was produced after Stearman had left, and that the aircraft was effectively a Boeing. Nevertheless, the name Stearman was perpetuated.

In 1934 the US Navy and Army Air Corps ordered the type. It was the first aircraft to meet both Navy and Army training requirements, thousands serving as the Navy NS and N2S, and Army PT-13 and PT-17. Production of the machine ran into five figures and, of these, three hundred built for the Royal Canadian Air Force were called Kaydets; for some reason this name has unofficially been associated with the aircraft of all the series. The production Model 75 had various power plants fitted, all of them being radial engines of about 220hp made by Lycoming, Continental or Jacobs. Many were exported.

The machine now owned by John Jordan, was one of the 8421 military trainers built at Wichita prior to November 1943 and was originally fitted with a 225hp Jacobs engine. John Jordan learnt to fly in the Royal Air Force and later, as a member of the Air Transport Auxiliary, he flew a very wide range of machines. He then joined an airline as a pilot and whilst flying with them he had to take over the family flour mill. When he was running this, John started a crop-spraying service in England along the lines of the ones in America, but the aircraft that he was using could not lift enough of the liquid. Whilst in Arkansas, USA, he came across the Stearman being used for crop spraying. Fitted with the powerful Pratt and Whitney R985 AN/1 Wasp Junior engine the Stearman could lift over half a ton of spray. It was shipped back to England in 1965, and registered as G-AROY became the mainstay of the crop-spraying business. In addition to the 450hp engine, the fuselage had been widened slightly to take the huge fibreglass tank which was situated in the front cockpit.

Another modification was the addition of a wire from the centre of the top wing to the fin. One of the dangers associated with crop spraying is the presence of low cables, and pilots engaged in such activities become adept at flying under them. When fully loaded, the Stearman flies slightly tail up, and after a couple of close shaves the wire was fitted to deflect the tail below any cables. Another problem is the occasional awkwardly placed tree, and on one occasion the machine flew through such a tree, without injury — at least to the aircraft!

The crop-spraying business went into decline and was wound up eventually; the aircraft were sold, but John Jordan kept G-AROY for his own use, flying from a field on a friend's farm. The machine is now only flown for fun, either privately or in public displays where its powerful engine can be seen pulling it into a loop from take-off.

Once when following a railway line whilst coming slowly back from an airshow in north-east England, John found himself being overtaken (or perhaps one should say undertaken) by one of the new high speed trains. As the train went along an embankment he flew down parallel to it and paced it: the airspeed indicator showed 140 knots. As he exchanged friendly waves with its driver, the train came screeching to a halt. It appears that a passenger had been worried by the strange noise accompanying the train and pulled the communication cord — the Stearman has a bit of a reputation for being noisy.

Stories about the exploits of the aeroplane and its pilot abound. On another occasion the aircraft developed engine trouble as he was coming back from an airshow; it was impossible to continue and after much searching, he brought it down in a field bounded by a river. He very rapidly began to run out of field and, despite violent ground looping, the machine came to rest on its nose in the mud and nettles at the edge of the river. The problem was due to the presence of some swimming-pool disinfectant which had been left in the containers that he had used in refuelling. It was soon put right and, had the propeller not been bent, he could have flown it out. Getting the machine back home also proved an interesting experience — but that's another story.

Boeing Stearman Model 75N1 Kaydet G-AROY was one of many which were modified for crop-spraying after being retired from military service. Its excellent performance and manoeuverability make it an attractive aerobatic machine at the many airshows it attends.

General Aircraft GAL 42 Cygnet G-AGBN

Designed in 1936 by Chronander and Waddington, the all-metal GAL 42 Cygnet was intended right from the start to be a vice-free, easy-to-fly-machine. It was powered by a 150hp Blackburn Cirrus Major II. Modifications introduced after the prototype resulted in the very characteristic appearance of the tricycle undercarriage, two-seat machine. The outbreak of war in 1939 put an end to its manufacture and of the ten production machines, five went abroad and five were impressed into the RAF to be used to familiarise Douglas Boston crews with tricycle undercarriage techniques.

The Strathallan Aircraft Collection's Cygnet was the third built, but the last one to be registered, as G–AGBN. It had been camouflaged when first painted, but the scheme incorporated its civil registration number when it was delivered to No 23 Squadron, RAF, at Ford on 2 July 1941. A few weeks later it was impressed as ES915 and went to No 51 Operational Training Unit at Cranfield. For a short time it was with Cunliffe-Owen Aircraft at Eastleigh. When it returned to Cranfield it was flown twice by Squadron Leader Guy Gibson who was No 51 OTU's Chief Flying Instructor. It passed through the hands of various RAF units, ending up with the Metropolitan Communications Squadron at Andover, Hampshire. It was owned by a long succession of people, some having the machine for as little as a month. One of the owners, a Mr Blair, entered G–AGBN, then painted bright blue, for the Grosvenor Challenge Cup in the National Air Touring Competition at Cranfield, but out of the twelve entrants it came in last.

In 1965 the aircraft came into the hands of Jack Pomper who bought it through his firm of J and T Robinson Limited. Jack flew regularly from Croydon and later from Biggin Hill for the next ten years. He describes it as a beautiful machine, and during those years it gave virtually no trouble, but a great deal of pleasure. It proved itself to be an all-weather machine and in every way seemed to live up to the expectations of its designers in being a vice-free aircraft. Even when conditions were so bad that all other aircraft were grounded, Jack Pomper would take-off for his regular Sunday flight. When he took the aeroplane over it was unpainted, but highly polished and he kept it in this condition until following one of the Certificate of Airworthiness renewals he was advised that though the highly polished bare metal looked superb, it was opening up the way for corrosion, and the aircraft would be better preserved under a couple of coats of paint. Thus, it was painted light blue.

Jack Pomper went over to France several times with the aircraft with no incidents. Moreover, there were only two occasions during ten years of flying when the machine gave him cause for concern. Once when flying back to Croydon from Shoreham, he felt a vibration coming through the airframe which gradually increased to such an extent that he had started to look for an emergency landing site. Suddenly it stopped, and since the engine and controls were functioning perfectly as usual, he continued the journey. On landing he found that the wind generator had fallen off. Situated in the starboard wing, this small propeller-driven generator is used to charge the batteries. Obtaining a replacement posed no problem. On another occasion a somewhat noisier vibration was felt and one of the exhaust tailpipes fell off.

Eventually Jack felt that perhaps *Anno Domini* was beginning to take a hold and that he should give up flying and he looked around for a new home for the Cygnet. He toyed with the idea of putting it in store, but really felt that such an aircraft should be flying. The Strathallan Collection expressed an interest in it and Sir William Roberts came to Biggin Hill to see the aeroplane. He was impressed, but did not wish to fly it then. It was agreed that if Jack could fly it up to Strathallan, he would buy it. That last five-hour flight, on 6 June 1975, was the longest and the saddest that Jack Pomper had in it, but at least the GAL 42 Cygnet would carry on flying. True to his word, Willy Roberts paid the £5000 on the nail and took possession of the world's last airworthy Cygnet.

Since Strathallan acquired the aircraft, it has been re-painted in its original camouflage scheme and flies regularly from the airstrip at Auchterarder. It seems a strange quirk of fate that this aircraft did not become one of the most popular light aircraft after the de Havilland 'Moths'.

Top: *The GAL.42 Cygnet which belongs to the Strathallan Aircraft Collection is a Mark II, differing from the Mark I in having a 150hp Cirrus Major; the Mark I had a 130hp de Havilland Gipsy Major engine.*
Right: *Cygnet G–AGBN flying over Perthshire.*

Hawker Hurricane MkIIB G-AWLW

Although often overshadowed by the Supermarine Spitfire, it was the Hawker Hurricane which bore the brunt of the fighting against the *Luftwaffe* during the Battle of Britain in 1940 and shot down more German aircraft than all other Allied types combined during the first year of the war. Designed by Sydney Camm, the Hurricane was the RAF's first monoplane fighter, the first eight-gun fighter to enter service in the world, and the first RAF machine to exceed 300mph in level flight.

In 1933, Camm had been working on a monoplane version of the Fury to be built around the Rolls-Royce Goshawk engine. However, Rolls-Royce were working on a new engine developed from the Kestrel, the PV12. This large V-12 engine had the makings of the ideal engine for the new generation of fighters, and Camm re-worked his original design to use this new engine. The prototype Hurricane K5083 first flew on 6 November 1935, powered by the PV12, now named Merlin, which drove a two-blade fixed-pitch propeller. Its structure was similar to the Fury's and very dissimilar to the Spitfire's monocoque. It had a tubular metal space-frame fuselage and engine bearers, with wooden stringers; fabric-covered ribs and formers contoured the rear fuselage; the nose cowlings were metal panels; the wing, built in three sections, was of metal spar and rib structure covered with fabric, and could accommodate eight 0.303in Browning machine guns. A canopy enclosed the cockpit. Despite trouble with the Merlin engine, K5083 showed exceptional promise, reaching nearly 315mph and climbing to 15,000ft in 5.7 minutes from take-off. Hawkers immediately made plans to mass produce the new fighters; their faith was rewarded when the government placed an initial order for 600.

The Hurricane Mk I entered service with No 111 Squadron, RAF, in October 1937. By August 1940, over 2300 had been delivered. The 'old fashioned' construction lent itself to rapid assembly and field repairs, being familiar to ground-crews.

The Hurricane was modified, but never drastically re-designed; the wings were given a metal skin to improve performance and strength to allow heavier armament. More powerful Merlins and more efficient propellers further increased performance.

The Hurricane Mk II had the more powerful Merlin XX engine, the Mk IIB was fitted with twelve machine guns in the wing, and the Mk IIC had four 20mm Hispano cannons. The Mk IID was equipped with two 40mm cannons for tank-busting. No Mk IIIs were made. In 1943 the Mk IV ground-attack Hurricane had a 'universal' wing that could take

several armament combinations. Navalised versions, the Sea Hurricanes, were produced. When production finished in 1944 over 14,000 Hurricanes had been made.

There are very few airworthy Hurricanes left; The Battle of Britain Memorial Flight has two and Shuttleworth's Sea Hurricane is nearing full restoration. In addition there is Strathallan's immaculate Hurricane Mk IIB, built in Canada by the Canadian Car and Foundry Co Ltd, Fort William, Ontario, in 1942 as a Mk IIB for the Royal Canadian Air Force. Powered by a Packard-built Merlin 29 it was taken on charge as 5588 by No 2 Training Command, and stored. In 1943 it went to Western Air Command, but was still held in store. In June 1943 it joined No 163 Squadron for Army co-operation duties in Sea Island, British Columbia, and while it was there it was re-designated Mk XII.

Very little happened to it after that and eventually in 1950 it ended up in reserve for display purposes at Portage La Prairie. It was finally disposed of in 1952 when, with only 86 hours, 40 minutes flight time, it was sold to Ajax Aircraft Parts Ltd. Subsequently, a local farmer bought the aircraft as a plaything for his children but Robert Diemert bought it in 1964 and set about re-building it, in the process fitting a Merlin 25 engine. The aircraft was flown in Canada as CF–SMI. In 1967 it was air-freighted to Britain where it was used for the film *Battle of Britain,* flying over 80 hours during the shooting. Afterwards it was registered as G–AWLW and bought by N A W Samuelson of Elstree, Hertfordshire.

Two years later, in 1971, it was sold to Sir William Roberts along with two Spitfires and became the first aircraft in what is now the Strathallan Collection. It was taken up to Auchterarder, Tayside, in 1972, where it was re-built. It flew again, piloted by Duncan Simpson, on 28 June 1973, and now appears in all the Strathallan flying displays. It is painted to represent an aircraft flown by Squadron Leader Archie McKellan, CO of No 605 Squadron, coded UP–A, and serialised P3308.

Top: *It was Sir William Roberts' desire to own a Hawker Hurricane which led to the foundation of the Strathallan Aircraft Collection when he bought G–AWLW, a Canadian-built Mark IIB in 1969.*
Lower: *The Strathallan Hurricane seen flying over Perthshire; the red-doped patches on the wing-leading edges cover the ports of the 12 Browning machine guns.*

Fairey Swordfish Mk II LS326

The Swordfish, or 'Stringbag', despite being out-dated, was one of the most famous and best loved of all the aircraft of World War II, and probably accounted for the destruction of more German and Italian shipping than any other single type of aircraft. This success was partly due to its high manoeuvr-ability and great stability at low speed, and to the fact that it operated out of reach of the better shore-based fighters.

The whole history of the Swordfish is surrounded by strange facts; not only outlasting its intended successor, the Albacore, but it was built before its progenitor. In 1930 an Air Ministry Specification S9/30 for a Fleet spotter-reconnaissance aircraft was issued, and, in response, Fairey started work on the S9/30, the aircraft from which the Swordfish originated; however, it did not fly until February 1934. Meanwhile Faireys were working on a private venture, the TSR I, a torpedo bomber for the Greek Navy, which first flew in March 1933, and in many ways closely resembled the final Swordfish. Unfortunately, it got into an uncontrollable flat spin and its pilot, C S Staniland, only just managed to bale out. However, despite this, Faireys were confident enough to continue development and were able to use the design to meet the later Air Ministry Specification S15/33, for a more advanced torpedo-spotter-reconnaissance aircraft. This aircraft was the TSR II, powered by a Bristol Pegasus. It first flew in March 1934, only two months after the original S9/30 machine. Testing continued on the latter, but the Ministry accepted the TSR II and the production models were named the Fairey Swordfish. The S9/30 was tested as a float-plane up to 1936 and then seems to have been forgotten.

Three marks of Swordfish were produced. The Mk I entered FAA service in July 1936. The Mk II had a strengthened metal lower wing that could carry rockets, and the Mk III was equipped with radar, carried in a radome between the undercarriage legs. The Canadian-built version, with an enclosed cock-pit, was unofficially designated Mk IV.

Shortly after the introduction of the Mk II, the Bristol Pegasus III engine was replaced by a 750hp Bristol Pegasus 30, driving a three-blade fixed-pitch propeller. Although some Swordfish were made at the Fairey factory in Hayes, Middlesex, the majority of the 2392 machines were built by Blackburns at Brough, the final delivery being made in 1944.

The battle honours of the 'Stringbag', as it became known, are legendary, the most famous being the attack on the Italian fleet at Taranto in 1940, the crippling of the German battleship *Bismarck,* and the suicidal torpedo attacks on the *Scharnhorst* and *Gneisenau* during their 'Channel Dash' in 1942. This last episode, in which all six Swordfish led by Lt Cmdr Eugene Esmonde — for which he was awarded a posthumous VC — were shot down on their torpedo run, ended its career as a torpedo bomber. It was relegated to shore-bases and escort carriers, performing invaluably as a coastal patrol reconnais-sance spotter, minelayer and anti-submarine aircraft.

There is now only one Swordfish flying and only three others in museums. The Fleet Air Arm Historic Flight includes LS326, a Mk II built by Blackburns in 1943. As with many old aircraft which are still airworthy, LS326 did not see active service. It was used for communications and training, based first at Culham near Oxford, and later at Worthy Down near Winchester, Hampshire. In 1945 she was one of the aircraft in the victory display in Hyde Park, London, and later that year Fairey acquired her again and she was kept at Heston.

On 28 May 1947 Fairey put her on the civil register as G–AJVH and painted her 'Fairey Blue' and silver. After a spell at Hamble, G–AJVH went to White Waltham for storage. However, stored aircraft often do not keep very well, and in 1954 Sir Richard Fairey gave orders that the aeroplane should be put back into flying condition. This involved a major re-build during which it was found that many new parts were required. Some were found and others, such as the rigging wires, had to be specially made. Despite the enormity of the task it was completed in a year.

In 1958 the film *Sink the Bismarck* was made and G–AJVH's civilian days were over. She was re-painted in authentic colours as LS326 again and given the code lettering 5A to represent Lt Cmdr Eugene Esmonde's aircraft which led the first attack on the battleship; she still bears these colours. When Fairey Aviation became part of the Westland Group the company presented the aircraft to the Royal Navy and she has flown regularly with the Historic Flight since then.

The Fleet Air Arm Historic Flight's Fairey Swordfish Mk II is the sole remaining airworthy example of this famous World War II torpedo-bomber, anti-shipping strike and submarine hunter aircraft. The Strathallan Collection acquired a Swordfish for restoration to airworthy condition in 1980.

Douglas A-26C Invader N3710G

From the outset the A–26 was intended to perform multiple combat roles and to be the successor to the A–20 Havoc, so three different prototypes were ordered in 1941, each with different armament. The first version to go into service was the A–26B which was intended for ground attack roles. It differed from its prototype by the replacement of the single 75mm nose cannon with six 0.5in machine guns, later increased to eight. Remotely controlled dorsal and ventral turrets housed two 0.5in guns each. The dorsal turret was designed to allow the pilot to lock its guns forward to increase head-on firepower. The bomb load was increased from 3000 to 4000 pounds, and wing fixtures could carry supplementary fuel, sixteen rockets or up to 2000 pounds of bombs. A further eight machine guns were available in under-wing packs if required.

Towards the end of 1944 the A–26B Invader appeared in Europe, where it was used with great effect against enemy supply columns and armoured reinforcements being brought up to confront the Allied advance on Germany. In 1945 it began to operate against the Japanese. Late in the European conflict the bombardier-nosed A–26C arrived. Although most of the Invaders still on order at the end of the war from Douglas' Long Beach, Washington and Tulsa, Oklahoma plants were cancelled, the A–26 went on to become the mainstay of the newly formed US Tactical Air Command. It also served with the French *Armée de l'Air* for several years.

With the Korean War the Invader was back in the front line from June 1950 until half an hour before the ceasefire on 27 July 1953. Nor was its aggressive career yet at an end. Vietnam saw its deployment against the Vietcong until 1963, when at last the veteran aircraft began to cause concern following a series of accidents. Undaunted, it soon re-appeared in an improved B–26K counter-insurgency version which was the outcome of complete airframe re-manufacture by the On Mark Engineering Company. Improved performance resulted from the company's experience in converting the old warriors for the executive market by the installation of a 2500hp Pratt & Whitney R–2800–103W radial engines and wing-tip fuel tanks.

Captain Don Bullock, then managing director of Euroworld, first made the acquaintance of Douglas A–26C Invader N3710G as a pilot with Aero Service Corporation, and flew the aircraft extensively on low-level geo-magnetic survey operations in Alaska. The aeroplane was no youngster, having originally seen service as 43–22612 in Europe in 1945 either with the US Ninth Air Force in France or the US Twelfth Air Force in Italy, returning to the United States a year later. As an A–26C, it basically resembled the A–26B, but featured a bombardier nose, housing only two 0.5in machine guns. It was powered by two 2000hp Pratt & Whitney R–2800–79 Double Wasps.

It remained in operational use with the US Air Force, possibly going to Korea. In June 1952 came its second European tour of duty, with the 126th Bomb Wing at Laon, in France. In 1955, returned to America, the aeroplane was declared excess and removed from the USAF inventory in 1957. A period of five years civil operation followed before its purchase by Aero Service in 1962.

The last phase in the Invader's career began when it was pensioned off from the survey company and Don Bullock acquired it and added it to his USAAF Memorial Flight to fly together with Boeing B–17G *Sally B*. The A–26 made its début in England at the Biggin Hill Air Fair in May 1978 and later that month at the Anglo-American Air Festival at Bassingbourn. Research was going on in order to trace the aircraft's early service history in more detail, when the aircraft was tragically destroyed in a crash at the Battle of Britain display at Biggin Hill on 21 September 1980.

Douglas A–26C Invader 43–26612 became renowned for its spectacular displays at air shows in the United Kingdom, flown by Don Bullock. Immaculately maintained and finished it was part of the Cavalier Air Force based at Duxford.

Vickers-Supermarine Spitfire LF Mk IXb G-ASJV

The Spitfire Mk IX was originally a stop-gap to counter the Focke Wulf Fw 190A which by 1942 had the measure of the Spitfire Mk V which equipped most RAF front-line fighter squadrons. The Mk IX was basically a Mk V with the more powerful Merlins 61, 63 or 63A, for general operating altitudes and fighter role, denoted by an F prefix to the Mk number; or the 66 or 70, for low (LF) and high (HF) altitude fighters respectively. Incorporating two-stage superchargers, using 100 octane fuel and providing 20 lb per square inch boost, they gave the Mk IX a top speed over 400mph and a service ceiling of 43,000 feet. External differences to the Mk V were a longer nose, four-bladed propeller, six exhaust stubs, and a symmetrical underwing layout produced by substituting a box, instead of an oval radiator under the port wing. It is often described as the acme of the Merlin-powered Spitfires in combat terms, and was produced in many variations and greater numbers than any other mark after the Mark V.

The Vickers-Armstrong factory at Castle Bromwich concentrated on the production of Mk Vs and then Mk IXs, many converted Mk Vs. In August 1943, Alex Henshaw, Chief Test Pilot, flew Spitfire LF Mark IXb serial number MH434 for the first time. Later that month it was assigned to No 222 Squadron at Hornchurch, where it flew its first operational mission on 19 August. Most of its 70 sorties during the next four months were on 'Ramrod'-type operations escorting daylight bombers over occupied France, Belgium and Holland, as far as the Spitfire's limited range permitted, to provoke enemy fighter retaliation, flown by Flight Lieutenant H P Lardner Burke, DFC, of South Africa. On 27 August, escorting USAAF Boeing B-17s over Mardyck, the squadron, as part of a wing, engaged nine Focke Wulf Fw 190s which were attacking the bombers and Lardner Burke damaged one and shot down a second in the ensuing dog-fight. Another Fw 190 fell to his guns near Nieuport while escorting Martin B-26 Marauders on 5 September, and three days later he shared the destruction of a Messerschmitt Bf 109F with fellow South African Pilot Officer Smik near Boulogne. Between January and March 1944 MH434 was transferred temporarily, along with the rest of No 222 Squadron's Spitfire Mk IXs, to No 350 (Belgian) Squadron who moved to Hornchurch, Essex, to continue as bomber escorts on short-range missions. MH434 flew again with No 222 Squadron for the last time in March 1944 before going on to 84 Group Support Unit as part of the pool of operational aircraft maintained to supply the squadrons of No 84

Group, Second Tactical Air Force, in the immediate post-invasion period, emerging to complete one operation with No 349 (Belgian) Sqn. During the return trip it was necessary to land at B.1 (Bazenville advanced airstrip) in newly liberated Normandy to refuel. In March 1945 it went into store at 9 MU and in 1946 to 76 MU, being moved by 47 MU after sale.

The second phase of the aeroplane's operational life began in 1947, when along with nineteen other Spitfires it was shipped aboard the SS *Rotti,* via Tilbury, Essex, and was delivered to the Royal Netherlands Air Force as H-105. Re-erected at Kalidjati, Indonesia, in late 1947, the Spitfires went into action against Nationalist forces, with No 322 Squadron, LSK (Luchtstrijdkrachten) from Semarang. H-105, later re-coded H-68, flew some twenty-five ground attack missions. A period operating against infiltrators in areas allotted to the Dutch after United Nations' intervention followed, before the situation improved to the point where the Squadron could return to the Netherlands, but not before H-68 had suffered a belly landing. Most of the eighteen surviving Spitfires went to *La Force Aérienne Belge* which used them for training after overhaul by Fokker. Identified as B-13 for Fokker's test flying, the hardworking Spitfire joined the Ecole Pilotage Avancé, Brustem as SM-41 where it remained in service until 1954. Several years with the firm of COGEA as a target-towing machine with the civilian registration OO-ARA were completed before the aeroplane was repatriated in 1963, by now powered by a Merlin 76 engine, and registered to Tim Davies at Elstree, Hertfordshire, as G-ASJV.

In January 1968 the Spitfire was bought by Group Captain T G Mahaddie to be used later that year in making the *Battle of Britain* film. The aeroplane now belongs to Adrian Swire, and is based at Wycombe Air Park (formerly Booker Aerodrome) near High Wycombe, Buckinghamshire, where it is maintained in aerobatic shape (up to 5G Positive) by Personal Plane Services. It has also appeared in the film *A Bridge Too Far,* in which it was flown by Neil Williams, and has been used for television commercial work. Regular pilots are Sqn Ldr Ray Hanna, ex-leader of the RAF's 'Red Arrows' aerobatic display team, David Morgan and Tony Bianchi.

Supermarine Spitfire LF Mk IXb G-ASJV is owned by Adrian Swire and based at Wycombe Park. The last airworthy Mark IX in the UK, it is one of the few airworthy veteran military aircraft with a well-documented active service record.

Curtiss P-40N-5 Kittyhawk N1226N

Because the P-40 was a successful adaptation of an existing airframe, that of the radial-engined P-36, it was immediately available for mass production when the USAAF placed an order on 27 April 1939. Evaluation batches had been ordered of Lockheed P-38s and Bell P-39s, but neither would be fully operational until well into 1941, so the Allison V-710-19-powered P-40, despite performance and armament shortcomings, was given the opportunity to prove its toughness and adaptability, serving in every World War II combat theatre.

Apart from USAAF service, early models entered RAF service as the Tomahawk Mk I, diverted from *Armée de l' Air* orders after France fell in June 1940, but were inadequate for the fighter role and were used for reconnaissance. The P-40B (Mk IIA) introduced four machine guns, more armour plate and self-sealing fuel tanks. The P-40C (Mk IIB), with six guns, became the mount of the only mercenary air force ever, the American Volunteer Group or 'Flying Tigers', which fought the Japanese in China, apart from serving with the USAAF, RAF, RAAF, SAAF, the Turks and the Russians.

Introduced in 1941, the fighter-bomber P-40D (RAF Kittyhawk Mk I) was powered by an Allison V-1750-39 and had a shorter, deeper nose. The P-40E (Mk IA) was similar. The Mks I and IA served with distinction with British units in the Western Desert, as had the Tomahawk Mk IIB. Experiments with a Rolls-Royce Merlin 28 in a P-40 in 1941 led to the Packard V-1650 Merlin-powered P-40F, but performance was only marginally improved. Subsequent models reverted to Allisons. On the P-40F and most later models the fin was moved back twenty inches to counteract increased torque. The P-40K and lightweight P-40L were similar to E or F airframes; both were used mainly by the USAAF. The P-40M, similar to the L, was produced solely for Commonwealth use as the Kittyhawk Mk III. Continuing concern over performance resulted in the considerably modified P-40N. Powered by a V-1710-81, 99 or 115, it was the fastest P-40, with improved climb and ceiling, and the most numerous and last production P-40.

The Confederate Air Force's P-40N-5 was originally a Royal Canadian Air Force machine, serialled 867, which, when it was put on sale by the War Assets Corporation, had flown only nine hours. Sold for $50 on 12 August 1947, to Robert Farrington, it was transported to Boeing Field, Seattle, Washington State, and registered N1226N. Soon after, title passed to Universal Aircraft and then to Robert Harmon of Nabnasset, Massachusetts, on 24 February 1951. On 1 June 1951 it joined a weather research operation, called Scholarship House, at Norman, Oklahoma, which already used several P-40s. Six years later N1226N changed hands for $300, when Isaac Newton 'Junior' Burchinall, a Baptist preacher, crop-duster, warbird flyer and instructor, installed it on his narrow dirt strip, west of Paris, Texas. From there he has run a checkout school for aspiring 'fighter' pilots and the Flying Tigers Air Museum, for twenty years. In late 1958 the P-40, by now finished silver with a shark's mouth nose art, suffered a landing gear collapse, damaging belly and propeller.

In this state the aircraft was purchased by another crop-duster. Glenn 'Bucket' Parker, Jnr, of Nederland, Texas, and after dismantling, was moved by truck to Parker's Airport, at Port Arthur, Texas. Here, during 1958-59 it was re-built, to be flown only briefly before being grounded after engine trouble, parked in the weeds by yet another crop-dusting owner, until Mike Dillon found it in 1968. Having paid the ever-increasing bounty of $800, Dillon began to spend real money on the old aeroplane, and a lot of time. With the airframe stripped down, at Sky Harbor Airport, Phoenix, Arizona, it was obvious that the P-40 was in worse shape than had been expected. A replacement Allison engine was discovered, and a brand-new Curtiss propeller. Sheet metal work was needed to graft a new P-40L QEC (Quick Engine Change) onto the P-40N airframe, which meant that everything in front of the firewall, except the engine, was not authentic. The Kittyhawk, painted bright red, flew once more in 1964 after five years on the ground.

In 1964 a fatal crash robbed the Confederate Air Force of their P-40 Kittyhawk, so they offered Dillon $12,000 and the much travelled N1226N moved to its present base at Harlingen, Texas. Now sporting the colours of the Flying Tigers — poetic licence for a late model P-40N-5 — it is one of the most popular aircraft in the Confederate Air Force, flown frequently at air shows by 'colonels'. Lloyd Nolan, Joe Jones and astronaut and former Bell X-15 pilot, Joe Eagle.

Right: Confederate Air Force's Curtiss P-40N N1226N in flight; it has its civil registration number on the starboard fin, the last two digits repeated on the fuselage.
Top: P-40N, with manufacturer's c/n 29629 on the port fin, in spurious colours of the AVG, which flew P-40Bs and Es.

North American P-51D-25-NA Mustang NL2151D

During 1940 the British Purchasing Council in the United States approached North American to design a fighter to fit the emerging pattern of the European air war. Eight machine guns and an inline engine were required, and, incredibly, within 102 days of detailed design work being begun, the prototype was rolled out on its widely spaced undercarriage legs, minus only its 1100hp Allison V–1710–F3R engine. The first batch which entered RAF service were found to be faster than any other current fighter, at low and medium altitudes, but deficient in performance above 15,000 feet, above which most combat took place, due to the engine having no supercharging. In 1942 Rolls-Royce fitted Merlin 60 series engines to four Mustangs which improved the performance beyond all recognition, particularly at high altitudes, putting 50mph on the top speed and 11,000 feet on the service ceiling.

Meanwhile the USAAF had evaluated the aircraft as the XP–51 and placed its first order, as the A–36, for ground-attack, and then as the P–51A fighter, but was quick to realise the increased potency when they too tried a Packard V–1650–3 Merlin in the airframe. The engine became standard for both American and British Mustangs, and the aircraft's combination of speed, manoeuvrability at all altitudes, long range and adaptability to many roles, such as low-level ground-attack, fighter-bomber, photographic reconnaissance, bomber escort and even defence against V–1 flying bombs, made it arguably the finest all-round fighter of the war. But it was in the long-range bomber escort role in which the Mustang excelled, gaining air superiority over Germany in 1944 for the bombers of the US Eighth Air Force. The P–51D introduced the teardrop canopy in 1944, which remained characteristic until the aeroplane was withdrawn from USAF operational service, after extensive action in the Korean war. In 1967 the ubiquitous Mustang, having remained operational almost continuously with various minor overseas Air Arms, reappeared in the USAF, assembled from stored components by the Cavalier Aircraft Corporation, in a counter-insurgency configuration.

In 1974 Californian businessman, Jack Flahery, retrieved a number of P–51 Mustangs from Salvador. They had originally been civilian aircraft, illegally exported in 1969 to take part in the infamous 'Soccer War' between El Salvador and neighbouring Honduras. One of these, registered as NL32FF for the ferry flight, was sold to the Canadian warplane collector Don Plumb, who, having stripped off the jungle camouflage evidently decided that the amount of work needed to complete the restoration was too great. When Gordon and Barbara Plaskett, of King City, California, offered to trade in their already airworthy P–51, Plumb parted with his and a disassembled, but rare, TF–51D dual-control, two-seat trainer, too. In fact the Plaskett's Mustang had itself been a wreck when they bought it from writer Richard Bach, and had only recently taken to the air again, thanks to the efforts of Dale Smith, their mechanic. Now presented with more work, Dale soon reduced the airframe of the latest P–51 to its main components, but left the wings attached to the fuselage. The engine was sent away for overhaul by Jack Cochran and the propeller to C & S Propellers. The re-build took hundreds of man-hours of painstaking work: all the metal of the wings and fuselage was stripped, inside and out, and zinc-chromated after careful inspection for corrosion; all wing and tail bolts were replaced; the fuel tanks were removed and cleaned; all the hundreds of feet of coolant, hydraulic and fuel lines were removed, to be cleaned or replaced; the airframe was completely rewired and a new instrument panel made and fitted; new hoses and clamps were installed in the windscreen; all control surface bearings were renewed and the old low-pressure oxygen system was removed.

With new avionics installed the re-assembled aeroplane was at last test flown, and as Gordon Plaskett put it: 'Everything worked so well that it scared me!' Dale Smith had done a wonderful job, and the time had come to put the shine on the apple.

Gordon and Barbara had decided to paint their P–51D, now registered NL2151D, to represent *Moonbeam McSwine*, a US Eighth Air Force Mustang credited with nineteen aerial victories which had been flown by one William T Wisner. Making every effort for complete authenticity they managed to track the pilot down in Mississippi. He had only recently given all the details to an aviation artist, and between the three parties an exact reproduction, down to the correct shade of 'deep blue' for the cowling, was achieved. It was a perfect job, and this opinion was shared by the judges at the Watsonville and Merced antique fly-ins where NL2151D took first prize in the Military Fighter category.

North American P–51D–25–NA Mustang NL2151D is painted to represent a 361st Fighter Group, US Eighth Air Force P–51D flown by W. T. Wisner, based in the UK and from December 1944 in Europe.

North American (TB-25N) Mitchell N9494Z

The North American B–25 Mitchell went straight into production, like the other successful entrant to the US Army Air Corps competition of January 1939, the Martin B–26 Marauder. After the first nine off the assembly line, zero dihedral on the outer wing sections was introduced, giving the bomber its gull-wing appearance.

The first units began to receive the B–25 Mitchells in 1941. The Americans used the bomber almost exclusively in the Pacific, although it later went to the RAF, Russia, Netherlands, China and Brazil. In December 1941 a Mitchell destroyed a Japanese submarine, pre-figuring, by this first success for the type, its later role as an anti-shipping gunship armed with a 75mm gun in the nose and fourteen 0.5in machine guns, designated B–25G and H. The famous 800 mile Tokyo raid led by Col James H Doolittle in April 1942, when B–25s flew from USS *Hornet* (CV–8), although mainly of psychological value, gave the aircraft a special significance in the annals of the Pacific war. Post-war many B–25 Mitchells continued in service with the USAF Strategic and Tactical Air Commands, before gradual relegation to training and personnel transport duties by the end of the 1950s.

Mitchell 44–29121 was manufactured by North American Aviation, Kansas City, and delivered to the USAAF on 12 March 1945. Too late to see combat duty, its first base was Lubbock Field, Texas, where it was to be used for proficiency flying, but it left for an Air Training Command (ATC) unit at Turner Field, Georgia, later that month. It remained with ATC, moving to Enid Field, Oklahoma, for advanced twin-engine training, and then, in the same role to Barksdale, Los Angeles, in December 1946. Here for a time it also fulfilled primary combat/tactical use before returning to ATC at Lubbock and the 3500th Pilot Training Wing in 1949. 44–29121 remained there for the rest of its service life, which was only seriously interrupted by a visit to the Birmingham Modification Centre in Alabama for conversion to TB–25N configuration.

In April 1958 the fourteen-year-old aeroplane retired to Davis Monthan Air Force Base, Arizona, for storage, until being authorised for reclamation and dropped from the Air Force inventory in December 1959. One year later the Mitchell was purchased by the National Metals Company of Phoenix, Arizona, and for the next ten years, as N9494Z changed hands five times, the last owner in this period being Filmways Incorporated of Hollywood with whom it appeared in the film *Catch*

22. In 1970 the B–25 joined the Confederate Air Force, to become famous as *Laden Maiden,* later passing to Wayne Turner and Michael Louis Zahn, coincidentally of Lubbock, Texas, and 'Colonel' John Stokes. In this guise it was painted light brown and wore the spurious serial 430925, forming part of his Warbirds of the World Collection at San Marcos.

When a number of B–25s were required for the making of another film, *Hanover Street,* in 1978, Jeff Hawke gathered five together with crews willing to fly them to location in England. (Hawke, with his partner David Tallichet of Long Beach, California, and the late Frank Tallman, have been responsible for virtually all the World War II veterans to appear on the screen during the last fifteen years, in films like *633 Squadron* and *A Bridge Too Far*.) In April, after a week's delay due to bad weather, they set out on a southerly ferrying route across the Atlantic via the Azores. One aircraft (N9115Z) was forced to turn back, and eventually made its own way via Greenland a week or two later, but the remainder (N7681C, N86427, N9494Z and N9455Z) arrived eight and a half hours later, after an eventful crossing during which they had been forced down to wave-top height by bad weather, and occasionally worried by the mechanical niggling of the old aeroplanes. N9494Z, as the only radio-equipped machine, naturally assumed leadership of the formation, which, after a stop-over in the Azores, made landfall in Portugal. From there the route lay via Jersey to Luton where the incipient 'stars' were painted Olive Drab, and assumed new identities, with Varga-style nose art, for their movie parts. N9494Z (now dubbed *Gorgeous George-Ann*) was able to supply the pattern, from her own original dorsal turret, for the props department to replicate turrets for the other aircraft, and also was fitted with a smoke-making device on her port engine. This aeroplane, remains now in England with N86427, fellow ex-CAF *Doolittle's Raiders.*

North American B–25J/TB–25N N9494Z has had an eventful career as a film 'star' and display aircraft since leaving USAF service. Named Gorgeous George-Ann, *she is pictured as she appeared for the film* Hanover Street. *She is registered to Doug Arnold of Warbirds of Great Britain and is based at Blackbushe.*

Boeing B-17G Fortress N17TE

In 1921 and 1923 Billy Mitchell demonstrated that a bomber could sink warships. The resulting warship versus bomber controversy merged with the controversy over the strategic air power, advocated by Mitchell, based on a long-range bomber force. When America eventually accepted the doctrine, the B–17 became its instrument. However, in 1934 it was still difficult to imagine that a threat to the United States' security would ever come at anything but sea level. The requirements of the 1934 US Army Air Corps' brief were for a multi-engined anti-shipping and long-range bomber. Boeing designed a four-engined prototype which averaged 252mph on its transcontinental delivery flight from King County Airport, Washington State, to Wright Field, Ohio, in August 1935. The Air Corps were pleased, although the prototype had crashed due to pilot error, and with the designation B–17, and named Flying Fortress, it went into production, but with a change from the original Pratt & Whitney R–1690E Hornet to Wright R–1820 Cyclone engines. By the outbreak of war in Europe less than one-third of the aircraft ordered had been delivered, but in 1940 twenty B–17Cs were diverted to the RAF as Fortress Mk Is in return for combat evaluation reports. The results of this led to self-sealing fuel tanks and increased armour in the B–17D. The B–17E had a supplementary tail gun turret, ventral ball turret, power-operated upper turret and flexible guns in the nose, upper fuselage and both beam positions — a total of eight 0.5in and one 0.3in machine guns aft of the cockpit. The bomber began to justify its name. The B–17E introduced the familiar large dorsal fin fillet. A total of 12,731 B–17s were built.

After the United States entered the war the B–17s of the Eighth Air Force, operating from bases in England, became the mainstay of the deep penetration daylight strategic bombing raids on occupied Europe and Germany, which began in August 1942, although the bomber also served with distinction in the Pacific.

The B–17 was viceless and forgiving, exceptionally stable in tight, high-altitude formation, and, alone at lower altitudes very pleasant to fly. It was also capable of sustaining battle damage few aircraft could approach.

Boeing B–17G, serialled 44-85784, was built at Burbank, California, by the Lockheed Aircraft Corporation's Vega subsidiary. She had the additional chin turret with two 0.5in guns for protection against frontal fighter attack, introduced on the G model. For conversion for Pacific duties the aircraft was delivered to Convair Air Force Base, Nashville, but the war ended before she could be ferried and it was 2 May 1948 before she was delivered, instead, to Wright Field, Ohio, to join a USAF Bombardment Squadron. There she remained for four years before being relegated to training duties at Shenectady, New York, and later at Hill Air Force Base, Utah, finally ending her USAF career at Olmstead AFB, New Jersey. There she was demilitarised and sold abroad for high-altitude survey work early in 1958.

Entered on the French register as F–BGSR the Fortress arrived at Le Bourget on 18 March 1958, to work with the Institut Géographique Nationale, Creil. Although minus turrets and bomb racks, the bomb doors and observation areas remained, and, basically, cameras replaced guns. In 1975 she was pensioned off again, but was immediately bought by Ted White Operations. White was a Director of Euroworld, an aircraft sales and ferrying company, which had already donated another ex-ING B–17 on permanent loan to the Duxford Aviation Society. Reregistered with the American FAA as N17TE, the intention was to fly their latest Fortress as an airborne memorial to the 79,000 American airmen who died in Europe during World War II. Her latest base is at Duxford, near Cambridge, from which, for the past four years, she has emerged to show her paces at airshows not only in Britain, but on the Continent, and has become famous for surprise appearances a few feet above the ground, wheels up, with no public warning. Usually it was Captain Don Bullock, the man who founded Euroworld, in the pilot's seat but Keith Sissons is now the regular pilot.

Nose art proclaims the B–17's name *Sally B,* and the aircraft is finished to represent a Fortress of the 749th Squadron, 457th Bomb Group, 1st Bomb Wing, US Eighth Air Force, stationed during the war at Glatton, near Huntingdon. She underwent a major overhaul in winter 1979, and is the last B–17 flying in Europe, and probably the last Vega-built machine flying anywhere. It costs over £2,400 to fill her tanks to capacity, highlighting the cost of keeping veteran aircraft flying. Her tanks hold 1,200 gallons and she consumes some 200 gallons per hour in flight.

Right: *The immaculate Boeing B–17G Flying Fortress Sally B is one of the most impressive sights at British air shows.*

Top: *Sally-B's Varga-style nose-art. The aircraft has no armament, or G-variant nose turret.*

Republic P-47N Thunderbolt N47TB

In 1940 Alexander Kartveli, chief engineer of the Republic Aviation Corporation, recognised that the European war was dictating new requirements for fighters, putting a premium on greater operational range, high service ceiling without loss of performance, speed, heavier armament and armour-plate protection for pilot and fuel tanks. Discarding the troublesome Allison V-1710 liquid-cooled inline engine adopted by Lockheed, Bell and Curtiss for their fighters, Kartveli re-designed his original Allison-engined fighter, the XP-47/47A, around the Pratt & Whitney XR-2800-21 Double Wasp radial engine and housed its 'washing-machine-sized' turbo-supercharger in the rear fuselage. It was designated XP-47B (XP for prototype, pursuit). It first flew on 6 May 1941. Another interesting feature was the inward-folding undercarriage which shortened by nine inches on retraction in order to provide adequate ground clearance, when extended, for the twelve-foot-diameter propeller, but allowed it to retract comfortably into the available wing space.

The first production batch of P-47Bs came out in March 1942, going to fighter training establishments in the United States, but a year later P-47Cs flew their first operational missions from England with the US Eighth Air Force. Officially name, Thunderbolt, their size, weight, power and ability to survive battle damage eventually earned them the affectionate nickname 'Jug', abbreviated from the earlier, less complimentary 'Juggernaut', when its looks and manoeuvrability had been compared unfavourably to those of the elegant Supermarine Spitfire. In fact, the qualities Kartveli had designed originally into the Thunderbolt meant that it was the first fighter able to escort high-level daylight bombers over Europe, catch and kill the Focke-Wulf Fw 190A and Messerschmitt Bf 109G in level flight and dive at speeds approaching Mach 0.9. Its low-level performance was unspectacular, but above 20,000 feet it was a fair match for the enemy. The most successful Eighth Air Force P-47 fighter group was the 56th, with several aces, including Robert Johnson and Francis Gabreski, the Eighth's joint top aces.

The P-47 served in the Far East with the USAAF and RAF mainly and with considerable success as a fighter-bomber, and in Russia under the Lend-Lease scheme. The P-47 was continually improved, but the water-injection R-2800-63 engine of the P-47D-10 and 11 produced the first major performance improvement. From the P-47D-25 onwards all sub-types had a teardrop canopy in place of the conventional 'glass-house' and familiar 'razor-back'

fairing of earlier models. Some two-thirds of the Thunderbolts produced survived World War II and went on to equip air forces all over the world.

In 1962 the 'colonels' of the Confederate Air Force spotted an advertisement in *Trade-a-Plane* offering five airworthy Thunderbolts for sale in Nicaragua, at $8000 each (or $11,000 fully armed). A fact-finding expedition showed that the elements were rapidly affecting the condition of the airframes. Back in Texas seven pilots each contributed $1250 and a working party returned to Nicaragua with the necessary equipment to get one of the aircraft into shape for a home flight. They must have chosen the best, because 44-53436 was the only Thunderbolt to make it back to the United States, two of the five having already crashed, and two more doing so later. Six days' work readied the P-47 for ferrying which was going to be a marathon flight for 'Colonel' Dick Disney. Last-minute efforts to obtain permission to overfly Mexico and land there failed, so he would have to fly 325 miles to Guatemala City, and from there more than 900 miles tracing the Mexican coast.

The Thunderbolt was a late model P-47N, which, as luck would have it, was designed for the World War II Pacific Theatre, and apart from a re-designed wing adding 22 inches of wingspan, carried additional fuel tankage. On 7 February 1963, Disney left for Guatemala City and reached Brownsville, Texas, with little trouble, despite the fact that few instruments were functional. At this time the aeroplane wore the Nicaraguan air force number 71, but it was registered in the United States as N478C.

The P-47N flew, somewhat unreliably, until, in 1970, Colonel Tom Holman of Vero Beach, Florida, assumed its sponsorship. At last it was stripped down for a complete overhaul and restoration. Tragically, on its third test flight the engine failed, due to carburettor problems and Dick Disney was compelled to force land short of the airport. The aeroplane crashed into tree stumps and suffered heavy structural damage, much to the dismay of the restoration crew. But Holman was made of as stern stuff as the Thunderbolt, and with great determination, and at further considerable expense, the aircraft was repaired. It now flies again, with the Confederate Air Force, registered N47TB, along with six more Thunderbolts since found in Peru.

Right: *Republic P-47N N47TB in echelon with a Hawker Sea Fury T Mk II and two P-51D Mustangs.*
Top: *N47TB seen at Harlingen in 1976 in natural metal finish.*

de Havilland Mosquito T Mk III G-ASKH

As with many of the most important aircraft of World War II, the seeds of the Mosquito — the DH98 — were sown before hostilities commenced in 1939. The famous wood-built DH88 Comet racer, developed for the London–Melbourne race, provided de Havilland with their experience in high performance twin-engined machines. This machine, conceived out of Geoffrey de Havilland's patriotic feeling that Britain should provide the winner of the England to Melbourne race, was of all-wood construction and was powered by two special Gipsy SK R engines.

The de Havilland Company, through their designer R E Bishop and his team, envisaged the DH98 as a high-speed unarmed bomber, powered by two Rolls-Royce Merlin engines.

Following their earlier experience with the DH88 Comet and the sleek, advanced DH91 Albatross airliner, the airframe construction was to be entirely of wood, for several reasons: war seemed inevitable and there would be heavy demand on the nation'a materials, especially metals (during the war Vickers-Supermarine even experimented with a 'plastic' Spitfire!). Also, by using wood, the construction of airframe components could be sub-contracted to firms not previously involved in aviation, thus easing the pressure on the already overloaded aviation industry. The Air Ministry was not impressed, and suggested that de Havilland would be better employed as sub-contractors on other work, but eventually they gave the go-ahead in 1939. The prototype, which had been built in secret at Salisbury Hall, near London Colney, Hertfordshire, had its first flight in November 1940. It was piloted by Geoffrey de Havilland, and, as expected, existing fighters could not catch it; during test flights, speeds around 400mph were recorded. Orders were quickly placed, and soon the first of the 7781 Mosquitoes were entering service, as unarmed, photographic reconnaissance aircraft with No 1 Photographic Reconnaissance Unit, at Benson, Oxfordshire.

Although originally designed as a bomber, the Mosquito was found to be highly versatile and was built for many roles: photo-reconnaissance (PR), fighter (F), night fighter (NF), bomber (B), trainer (T), target tug (TT) and, experimentally, torpedo fighter (TF); Sea Mosquitoes were also built. Forty-three marks were designated, some built only in Canada and Australia, but some did not go into production. The performance figures varied considerably from mark to mark. The early fighters had a maximum speed of 370mph, while the PR Mk 34 could reach 425mph. Production ceased in 1950.

The Mosquito became famous as a low-level pinpoint bomber, able to outrun enemy fighters — its designed role. Its most noted raids as such were on the Gestapo headquarters at Aarhus and Copenhagen, Denmark, on 31 October 1944 and 21 March 1945 respectively, destroying records on resistance activities; and on Amiens goal, allowing the escape of French resistance workers. They also spearheaded the RAF's Pathfinder Force, dropping marker flares on targets and 'conning' in the bomber force.

Post-war some went into civilian use, but they have gradually been written off. Now there are only three left flying, one of which is to be brought back to Britain from the United States, the second is at Strathallan, and the third is owned by BAe.

The latter aircraft was built in Leavesden in 1945 as RR299, as a T Mk III (the designation became T3 in 1946), a dual-control trainer generally similar to the NF Mk II. It went to No 51 Operational Training Unit at Cranfield in April 1945; then in December of that year it went out to Egypt and served with No 114 Squadron in Aden and Nairobi, returning in 1947 to Gosford.

In 1949 it served with No 204 Advanced Flying School at Driffield, East Yorkshire, then, following stays in various maintenance units it went to the Home Command Examining Unit at White Waltham in May 1957. In 1959 it went to Fighter Command Squadron at Bovington and joined No 3 CAACU (Civil Anti-Aircraft Co-operation Unit) at Exeter two months later.

In July 1963 it joined Hawker Siddeley, coming on to the civil register as G–ASKH. It was used for the films *Mosquito Story* and *633 Squadron,* but about that time one of its engines developed a fault and spares were difficult to obtain. The engine was replaced by one from an Avro York once owned by the Lebanese Trans-Mediterranean Airways.

Although on the civil register, G–ASKH is flown in standard war-time camouflage as RR299, but the squadron markings, HT–E, are spurious, being from *633 Squadron.* It is flown very gently these days only in good weather and keeping well within its performance limits as it is the intention of British Aerospace to keep it flying as long as possible. Spares are a problem, so the less Harry Robbins, who services it, has to replace, the better.

de Havilland Mosquito T Mk 3 RR299, owned by BAe and based at Hawarden, appears at several UK airshows. It is pictured at Biggin Hill.

Nord 1002 Pingouin G-ATBG

Following her defeat in World War I, Germany was not allowed under the terms of the Treaty of Versailles, to make military aircraft, but few restrictions were placed on civil machines. Under the guise of 'club machines', or sporting aircraft, Germany's aeronautical engineers were able to develop aircraft design and manufacturing techniques which, when the time came, could be turned to military machines.

The inter-war period was also the great era of air races and rallies which did much to stimulate the aircraft industry and it was in this connection that the Bayerische Flugzeugwerke AG (BFW) at Augsburg, of which Professor Willi Messerschmitt was director, was given a contract for a light aircraft to take part in the fourth *Challenge de Tourisme International* in 1934. The aircraft, known then as the M37 and designed by Willi Messerschmitt, was a breakthrough in design and formed the basis of the Bf 109. Instead of building a self-supporting rib and stringer type framework and then covering it in a structurally useless fabric or plywood skin, Messerschmitt adopted monocoque, stressed-skin construction: the metal skin was part of the load-bearing structure on both the fuselage and the wing. This resulted in a lighter and stronger airframe. Rationalisation in the German aviation industry resulted in the allocation of the letters 'Bf' to all aircraft from the BFW and thus the M37 became the Bf 108. BFW went bankrupt and became Messerschmitt AG, shortly after the Bf 109 design was begun. (Designs conceived by the new company had the new designation prefix Me; but aircraft designed by BFW retained the Bf prefix, including the Bf 108, Bf 109 and Bf 110.)

The Bf 108 had a retractable main undercarriage and a tailwheel and was originally powered by a 225hp Hirth engine, later replaced by the 240hp Argus As 10C. The wings were of single spar stressed-skin construction with automatic leading edge slots and trailing edge flaps. Initially, the control surfaces were dynamically unbalanced, but later modifications introduced aerodynamic balancing to the rudder and elevators.

The design had a few initial setbacks but in 1937 the aircraft won second place in the Oasis rally; in 1938 it claimed three firsts and a second in various international rallies and in 1939 it set a class altitude record of 29,766 feet and was the subject of a quite intensive publicity campaign.

It became a very popular machine, used by both the *Luftwaffe* and civilian organisations, and during the war 885s were built, mainly at the *Société Nationale de Construction Aéronautique* (SNCA) du Nord plant at Les Mûreaux. After the war Nord continued production, designated Nord 1000 series, producing the Nord 1001 Pingouin I and the Nord 1002 Pingouin II; the 1001 had a 240hp 6Q 10, and the 1002 had a Renault 6Q 11, replacing the Bf 108's 240hp Argus As 10C. These saw service in the French Navy (*Aéronavale*), being used for communications and training. The tricycle undercarriage successor to the Bf 108, the Bf 208, was built by Nord as the Nord 1101.

It is one of the *Aéronavale*'s Nord 1002 which is now flying as Lindsay Walton's G-ATBG. Built in 1945 it was used by the *Aéronavale* in the south of France as F-OTAN-5 before it was 'civilianised' as F-BGVX, when it joined a flying club at Pointoire, near Paris. In 1965 it was brought over to Elstree, Hertfordshire, and registered as G-ATBG and two years later Lindsay took it over.

Lindsay Walton is a farmer in north Cambridgeshire and learnt to fly privately some twenty years ago. Having previously flown a Miles M.38 Messenger he bought the Nord purely for the experience of flying it. He has a Piper which is his 'hack' machine. The Nord is an enjoyable aeroplane to fly (he describes it as a 'noisy Chipmunk') and it is also a thirsty one. The Renault 6Q 10 engine uses up twelve (Imperial) gallons of fuel an hour.

The machine is not without its problems, at least in upkeep. Spares are not so easy to find, and now he has resorted to buying two other machines in order to keep G-ATBG in the air. One of the main problems is the engine which has a habit of cracking the crankcase; he is now using his third and future supplies now seem limited!

Until 1979 the machine flew in spurious *Luftwaffe* desert camouflage, coded AT + BG, but the scheme was then changed to pale blue lower surfaces and sides and grey/green camouflaged upper surfaces. The insignia on the nose, a crying owl with a rolled up umbrella, representing Neville Chamberlain, was used by Mölders' *Geschwader*. This scheme was done for the BBC film *A Moment in Time* in which the aircraft appeared. It is really only through television and film work and air shows that the Nord can be kept in the air. Lindsay appears at between thirty and forty air displays a year, travelling as far afield as Strathallan and Belgium.

Lindsay Walton's airworthy Nord 1002 Pingouin G-ATBG is based at Sutton Bridge where he also stores two others, G-ASTG and G-ASUA, for spares. Rear windows are painted out to represent a Bf 109 for a film.

Avro Lancaster 'B' MkI PA474

The Avro Lancaster was a four-engined re-design of the unsuccessful twin Vulture-powered Manchester of 1940, both developed under the direction of Avro's chief designer, Roy Chadwick. The prototype Lancaster flew on 9 January 1941. The choice of the Rolls-Royce Merlin XX engine for the Lancaster and the careful attention paid to the problems of future field servicing contributed to its reliability in squadron service. The wing was of all-metal stressed-skin construction, built in five sections: the rectangular centre section, integral with the fuselage; two tapering outer sections; and two wing-tip sections. Leading and trailing edges were separate assemblies. The semi-monocoque fuselage comprised five main parts. The Lancaster had a huge bomb-bay designed to carry 4000 pounds of bombs in various configurations, but during the war this was progressively increased to accommodate 8000, 12,000 and then 18,000 pounds, and, with modifications, the 12,000 pound 'Tallboy' deep-penetration bomb, and finally, the 22,000 pound 'Grand Slam' earthquake bomb. Lancasters will, of course, always be associated with the special 'dam-busting' 'bouncing' bomb designed by Barnes Wallis, and used by No 617 Squadron, led by Wing Commander Guy Gibson to destroy the Möhne and Eder dams on 17 May 1943.

After the German surrender in May 1945, Lancasters delivered thousands of tons of food to the Netherlands and flew home 74,178 Allied ex-prisoners of war, but the 'Lanc' is still remembered as the most outstanding British bomber of World War II, playing the main part in the RAF's devastating area bombing night attacks on German cities.

The Lancaster which flies with the RAF Battle of Britain Memorial Flight was built by Vickers Armstrong at Hawarden, near Chester, in 1945 as a basic B Mk I. Modified for Far Eastern operations with 'Tiger Force', the dorsal turret was removed to accommodate an additional, external saddle fuel tank. The sudden end of the war with Japan, however, prevented the aircraft from going into action. In 1947 Lancaster PA474 was earmarked for photo-reconnaissance conversion, modifications being completed by the end of August, including deletion of all turrets. It was re-designated PR Mk I. A year later it joined No 82 Squadron, and was coded M. Within the next few years the Squadron's PR Mk Is completed a 1,216,000 square mile photographic survey of Central and East Africa. In 1952 the aircraft returned to England and was put out on loan to Messrs Flight Refuelling for trials. In April 1954 it transferred to the Royal Aircraft Establishment,

Cranfield, for more experimental work on laminar flow swept wing trials, being conducted by Handley Page in connection with the HP 115 project, necessitating fitting a vertical dorsal wing/fin attachment. PA474 retained its No 82 Squadron code letter.

In October 1963 the Lancaster was adopted by the Ministry of Defence Air Historical Branch and flown from the RAF Museum repository at Henlow in August 1965 to Waddington. It was restored to become a memorial for RAF Waddington, appropriately the base of No 44 (Rhodesia) Squadron, the first to receive Lancasters in early 1942. It was painted and coded to represent KM–B (R5508), the No 41 Squadron machine in which Squadron Leader J B Nettleton led the heroic Augsburg daylight raid on 17 August 1942, winning a posthumous VC.

In 1973 the Lancaster joined the Battle of Britain Memorial Flight at Coltishall, and that same year the Ministry of Defence received a 20,000 signature petition, organised by the Lincolnshire Lancaster Committee chaired by Mrs Hilda Buttery, requesting the aircraft be stationed in that county, from which so many had flown during the war. Since 1975 the port side of the nose has borne the Arms of the City of Lincoln, whose citizens had adopted the bomber.

Eventually a move was made to Lincolnshire, and the Battle of Britain Flight has been stationed at Coningsby, since March 1976. That year also saw the restoration of the mid-upper turret, astrodome and functioning bomb doors. A Warwickshire businessman, travelling in Argentina, had spotted a turret on a practice range. It was eventually presented to the RAF and the Royal Navy shipped it home aboard HMS *Hampshire*. The staunch members of the Lincolnshire Lancaster Committee again stepped in to provide the funds, and a fairing was hand-made and fitted by Mariner Engineering of Grimsby.

From 1977 to 1978 the old bomber was grounded while some 100,000 corroded magnesium alloy rivets were drilled out and replaced and a corroded fuel tank from each wing removed to be copied and replaced at the next major overhaul. Early in 1979 fuel checks and ground runs led to a test flight programme which satisfied the Battle of Britain Flight that PA474 could return to the airshow circuit, as Nettleton's B Mk I. In 1980 it was coded AJ-G, the code of Gibson's Dam's Raid B Mk I Special.

PA474 is not pure to one Lancaster mark; the aim is to keep it flying in accurate but not exact condition. It has three Merlins Mk 502s and one T24. It is restricted to a +2G limitation.

Hawker Sea Fury Mk11 TF956

A glance at collected drawings or photographs of World War II aircraft will show that, by and large, British fighters have inline, water-cooled engines. The pros and cons of the two engines can be argued at great length, but for the early part of the war the British were generally not in favour of air-cooled radials, mainly because of the availability of the excellent Rolls-Royce Merlin. However, in 1942 a Focke-Wulf Fw 190A was captured. This aircraft, powered by a BMW 1700hp air-cooled radial engine had a top speed of 382mph and was noticeably superior to the Supermarine Spitfire Mk V, then the standard RAF fighter. It has been claimed that this comparison caused the authorities to re-assess the radial engine.

In 1942 the Air Ministry issued Specification F6/42 for an aircraft developed from the Hawker Tempest. The Tempest, a laminar-flow wing development of the Typhoon, was one of the fastest aircraft used by the RAF. The Fury, emerging to Specification F2/43, was in a way a lightweight re-design of the Tempest. The laminar-flow wing was retained but Camm re-designed the centre-section integrally with the monocoque fuselage. Prototypes were flown with the Griffon and the Sabre, but it was the rapidly developing Bristol Centaurus radial that was finally chosen. The Tempest Mk II was also powered by the Centaurus. The first flight of the Fury, powered by a Griffon engine, was in 1944, but the RAF, however, withdrew its orders for the Fury, and, as far as Britain was concerned, it was the Royal Navy which, requiring a high-performance, carrier-based fighter-bomber, provided the navalised adaptation of the Fury, the Sea Fury, with enough orders for it to become one of the most impressive aircraft of its era.

Boulton-Paul was nominated to produce the Sea Fury, but had completed only a prototype, which flew in February 1945, before the end of World War II, when Hawker took over production. Hawker built two prototypes, SR661 and SR666 (the latter a fully navalised aircraft) powered by Bristol Centaurus XV engines, driving five-blade propellers. The F Mk X entered production in 1946, featuring a 248hp Centaurus 18 engine and a four-blade propeller; 50 were built. The FB Mk 11, with a five-blade propeller and improvements, entered FAA service in 1946.

The Sea Fury became the standard Fleet Air Arm fighter-bomber. A total of 860 machines was produced, of which the FAA received the large majority and the others went to Australia, Burma, Canada, Cuba, Egypt, West Germany, Iraq, Netherlands and Pakistan. The Sea Fury was the standard combat aircraft of the Australian, British and Canadian naval air arms in the Korean conflict and although initially deployed in ground-attack roles they proved their worth against the MiG–15 jet fighters, Lieutenant P Carmichael of No 802 Squadron, operating from HMS *Ocean,* claiming the first Fleet Air Arm MiG–15 kill on 9 August 1952. The Sea Fury was declared obsolete by the FAA in 1956.

The Sea Fury's maximum service speed was 460mph which was only slightly lower than that of the fastest piston-engined aircraft to enter service with the RAF, the de Havilland Hornet which had a maximum speed (first production model) of 472mph. Indeed an American-owned Sea Fury holds the world speed record for a piston-engined aircraft at 520mph.

The Fleet Air Arm's Sea Fury FB Mk 11 was built by Hawker Aircraft in 1946 and entered service in 1947, serialled TF956. It served in No 802 Naval Air Squadron at various air stations and then went to Korea with No 807 Squadron operating from HMS *Theseus.* The machine flew on some two hundred operational sorties, totalling two hundred and thirteen hours. Although she was hit by flak on more than one occasion it appears from the records that she was never damaged badly enough to warrant major repairs.

TF956 spent some time in No 738 Squadron and No 1834 (RNVR) Squadron and was retired in 1954. In 1960 the aircraft was allotted to Airworks Ltd for fleet requirement duties and then in 1963 Hawkers re-purchased her, initially for re-sale abroad, but then they decided to restore her, in order to join Hawker's 'Historic Aircraft'. Pressure of work due to development of the Hawker Harrier caused her restoration to be suspended and eventually in 1971 she was offered back to the Fleet Air Arm who completed the restoration and TF956 joined the FAA Historic Flight, based at RNAS Yeovilton, in January 1972.

The Fleet Air Arm Historic Aircraft Flight's Hawker Sea Fury FB Mk 11, TF956, is finished in the markings it bore during the Korean War of 1950–53, when operated by No 807 Squadron, FAA from the carrier HMS Theseus. TF956 was regularly flown by Chris Johnson, but is now flown by Lt Cmdr L. Wilkinson, CO of the Historic Flight.

Miles M.65 Gemini IA G-AKKH

The M.65 Gemini was the last of the line of Miles aircraft in the tradition of the M.3A Falcon, M.17 Monarch and M.38 Messenger. A four-seat, twin-engined, low-wing cabin monoplane, evolved in 1945 from the M.38 Messenger,,and using a similar wing and fuselage, the Gemini's structure followed the Miles 'hallmark' of plywood over spruce spars and ribs. The prototype flew on 26 October 1945 but with a fixed undercarriage to allow it to be demonstrated as early as possible. It had a distinctive twin-finned tail unit. The next demonstration model, designated 1A, was fitted with a retracting main undercarriage which folded back under the engine nacelle. During the next twelve months 120 were built and a further ten were ready to be assembled at a later date. The Gemini 1A, 1B and 4 had Cirrus Minors, the 3, 3A, 3B and 7 had Gipsy Majors, while the Gemini 8 had Cirrus Majors. One of the first aircraft was G–AILK which made the first post-war solo flight to Australia, piloted by Group Captain A F Bandidt, an Australian, arriving there in January 1947.

The Gemini was a great success, and a total of 170 was built. As a four-seat, twin-engine luxury machine it had few equals and was used in instructional and executive roles by commercial as well as private operators. Its attractiveness lay in its friendly, almost cosy appearance, and the luxury of the cabin in which the four occupants found themselves accommodated. It was also great fun to fly and exceedingly reliable. The Gemini was developed into the M.75 Aries.

Although not designed for racing, Geminis were entered in races, but without a great deal of success. Some honours were won, however, by Fred Dunkerley's G–AKKB, and the same aircraft won the Siddeley Challenge Trophy in 1953. Nat Sommers in his modified Gemini 3, among other successes, won the 1949 King's Cup Air Race.

Many of the Geminis went abroad and one which ought to have gone was OO–CD. Apparently bought by A Fischer and Co Ltd, it should have gone to the Belgian Congo. However, plans seem to have been changed and in 1948 it was registered to A F Bandidt, as G–AKKH, but a year later it became the property of S Bourne & Company of Nottingham and for the next fourteen years it was in regular use. From about 1963 the aircraft flew less frequently until finally it was withdrawn from use in 1968. Two years later it was acquired by Shobden Aviation Company.

In 1977 Mike Russell needed a fine pitch propeller for a DH82 Tiger Moth which was to be used for towing the vintage gliders of the Russavia Collection. The search for this took him to Shobden airfield and,

having purchased the propeller, he wandered round a hangar. He noticed an aircraft for which he had always had a soft spot, the Miles Gemini, dusty and unused at the back of the hangar. After enquiries he was told that the Shobden Aviation Company might be persuaded to part with it. Negotiations were started and eventually the machine was bought by Mike Russell.

Mike had learnt to fly gliders as a boy at Dunstable, Bedfordshire, and since then flying has been his life, first in the RAF and then as a captain in commercial airlines. His enthusiasm is such that his collection of vintage gliders has grown into the Duxford-based Russavia Collection, and in one way or another all his time is spent involved with aviation.

The Gemini, known to Mike's family and friends as Gemima, had not seen much use for some years although it had been entered, not very successfully, in the 1972 Strongbow race, which accounts for the '142' painted on the tail and wing. Mike flies it purely for pleasure, both for himself and for others who appreciate such things, sometimes privately and at other times in public displays. Recently it has been grounded because of a fault in the undercarriage which on close investigation turned out to be a manufacturing fault which had been a bit late in making itself known! A new undercarriage has now been manufactured and fitted. There was also a problem with the ignition on the port engine, but as Mike says, the aeroplane is in an 'active retirement'. The most important thing is to maintain it in as near perfect condition as possible, so rather than rush things in order to display her, the wiring harness is being carefully checked before the next Certificate of Airworthiness is applied for. One thing is certain, however, G–AKKH, or Gemima, will be flying for as many more years as possible.

G–AKKH, a racing version of the Miles M.65 Gemini, is currently registered to Shobden Aviation Company, Bristol and owned by Mike Russell, and is based at Lulsgate. It is one of very few twin-engined aircraft appearing on the airshow circuit.

Fairey Firefly AS Mk 5 WB271

The Firefly was the result of a continuous programme of development of machines for the Fleet Air Arm, but it was not a definite progression from another machine, although in some respects it is similar to the Fairey Fulmar. The engines used in the Firefly were from the Rolls-Royce Griffon series which were more powerful than the Merlins used in the Fairey Fulmar and the early Fairey Barracudas, and the aerodynamics were considerably more sophisticated. In order to retain control at low speeds, which is very necessary for a carrier-borne aircraft, the machine was fitted with Youngman flaps. These flaps, situated inboard of the ailerons, could be extended in three positions for take-off, landing and improving control at low speed. Not only the angle with the mainplane was changed, but also the position of the flap in relation to the mainplane. They differed from the Youngman flaps on the Barracuda by being fully retractable to improve high speed performance, and could not be used as dive brakes.

The wings, which were almost elliptical in shape, folded up and back to lie along the rear fuselage for stowage on carrier hangar decks. In the early marks these had to be folded manually by a ground crew, but the Mk 5 introduced power folding. The radiators, located under the engine in the early marks, and later Mk 7, were positioned in the wing root leading edges of the Mks 5 and 6.

Work started on the Firefly in 1935 and, by the end of 1941, the first prototype had flown, piloted by Chris Staniland, who was killed the following year in the second prototype. The Firefly remained in production until 1955 by which time over 1700 had been made, mainly by Fairey, but some by General Aircraft. The aircraft were designated by a role, the initials for these roles prefixing the mark, of which there were eight. Fleet Air Arm Fireflies saw active service in the Far East, the Pacific and Norway during the closing stages of World War II, and six squadrons were operational in Korea. They were also in action in 1954 against the communist terrorists in Malaya.

The aircraft which is now part of the Fleet Air Arm's Historic Flight is WB271, an AS Mk 5 (anti-submarine Mk 5), built in 1949 by the Fairey Aviation Company. It joined No 814 Squadron, FAA, based at Wildrose. It went to the Royal Navy Repair Yard at Fleetland and then saw service in the Far East and Korea, before joining the Royal Australian Navy, and flew from HMAS *Sydney*. In 1957 it was converted for target towing and served at Royal Australian Naval Air Station, Nowra, New South Wales, until March 1966.

In October 1966 Hawker de Havilland, who had now acquired it, put it up for disposal and while it was parked in the open at Bankstown WB271 was discovered by the Commanding Officer of No 814 Naval Air Squadron, Lieutenant-Commander Apps. He set wheels turning to acquire WB271 for the FAA Museum, and eventually, after high-level negotiations, the aircraft was purchased for £160, partly funded by the officers of HMS *Victorious,* and taken by road to Sydney to be winched aboard *Victorious*. She was left at Royal Naval Air Station Sembawang in Singapore to be repainted in its original Korean War colours. *Victorious* picked her up in 1967 and on return to Britain WB271 was presented to the FAA Museum at Yeovilton, Somerset.

After some years on static display it was decided to renovate the aircraft so that it could join the Historic Flight. In comparison with many other restorations the work was completed very quickly and the aircraft made its first flight seven months later in September 1972. However, over the following months WB271 was stripped again, repainted in Korean War colours and generally refurbished. Its first official flight was to retrace the path of the first pre-production (F5474) Firefly, Z1830, from Heathrow — then Fairey's factory airfield — to Yeovilton, Somerset, exactly thirty years earlier on 4 March 1943.

In 1974 it was found that the Griffon 74 engine was showing signs of serious cylinder corrosion and unfortunately spares for this engine are few and far between. However, with the help of the Royal Aircraft Establishment, Farnborough, enough spares from a Griffon 57 engine out of an Avro Shackleton were found to get the Firefly in the air again. For the want of another designation the new 'hybrid' engine had been designated Griffon 574.

Right: The FAA Historic Aircraft Flight's Fairey Firefly AS Mk 5, WB271, is currently the only airworthy Firefly in the world, following the loss of the Canadian Warplane Heritage's AS Mk 6 when it crashed into a lake.

Top: A close-up reveals the port wing folding and undercarriage attachment points, and shows the split radiators in the wing root which distinguished the Firefly Mks 5 and 6.

Chance Vought F4U-7 Corsair N33714

Ordered in 1938 the prototype Corsair, XF4U-1, flew on 29 May 1940, and became the first American aircraft to exceed 400mph in level flight. The wings were of inverted gull configuration to give the large propeller ground clearance, while permitting a short undercarriage required for carrier operations and reducing the height of the folded wings, aiding storage. Fulfilment of the initial order was delayed while the intended production F4U-1 was modified for mass production and alterations were made as a result of reports of air fighting in Europe which suggested fundamental changes to American concepts of armament and range. Six 0.5in wing-mounted machine guns replaced its two nose-and two wing-mounted 0.5in machine guns. The main fuel tank was moved from the centre section to the forward fuselage, pushing the cockpit back three feet, which had a very adverse effect on the pilot's view. After tests aboard USS *Saratoga* in 1942, carrier landings were ruled out, because of problems including the pilot's poor view and a tendency to 'bounce' dangerously on landing, so this naval fighter initially operated from land. Armour plate and self-sealing fuel tanks were adopted and the 2000hp Pratt & Whitney R-2800-8W Double Wasp radial engine became standard.

Corsairs first saw action with the US Marine Corps VMF-124 over Bougainville on 13 February 1943; by mid-summer land-based Naval squadrons were operating them in the Pacific. Vought joined with Brewster and Goodyear to meet increased demand for Corsair production. The F4U finally became a carrier-borne fighter in 1944, first in the hands of the Royal Navy, followed by the USN on 28 December 1944. The British machines had a wingspan reduced by sixteen inches to facilitate storage in the smaller RN carriers. It is generally regarded as one of the best US fighters produced during the war, and certainly the best carrier-borne fighter: it had a victory to loss ratio of 11:1. In the Pacific the Corsair became known as 'Whispering Death' by the Japanese, partly by virtue of the sinister whistle of the airflow through its cooler inlets.

The Corsair was in production longer than any other American military aircraft of this period. In the ten years until 1952 when production ceased, 12,571 were built and many variants introduced, some seeing notable service in Korea, with US forces, and others serving with the French *Aéronavale*.

In the early 1960s the US Marine Corps approached the French Government, which was just retiring the *Aéronavale*'s F4U-7 Corsairs, after long service in the Middle East and Algeria. Although this particular sub-type was exclusively used by the French, a specimen was obtained and stored for future display in a planned USMC museum. Dean Ortner, however, a mid-west cargo airline operator, was not only aware of the number of earlier model Corsairs gathering moss on several small airports around the country, but he had one of the type operated by the Marines in storage himself! Knowing that the ex-French machine was more or less airworthy, he offered to do a trade; the USMC agreed, and Ortner flew home in his latest acquisition.

When some time later he was tragically killed stunting a North American T-6 at an airshow the Corsair became the property of John Schafhausen, of Heyden Lake, Washington. He had been a Navy pilot during the war, had just completed a very expensive restoration of North American P-51 Mustang NL921, and was a director of Warbirds of America, the group of flyers and preservers of military aircraft. Schafhausen put in some work on the F4U-7 and gave it a new paint job and it became the Naval representative of his collection.

During the early part of 1976 plans were being made in Hollywood to produce a semi-fictitious series for television, based upon the exploits of the World War II US Marine Corps fighter ace Colonel Gregory 'Pappy' Boyington, starring Robert Conrad. Frantic searches turned up a motley collection of contemporary aircraft, including seven Corsairs. John Schafhausen and his aeroplane were chosen to lead the flying, he because of his skill as a pilot, and his machine because of its excellent condition. They flew many hours for the cameras, which captured some of the best aerial footage ever of the Corsair, from a base at Van Nuys in California. The series, entitled *Baa-Baa Blacksheep,* ran for two seasons and after its completion John flew his now famous Corsair back to home base. There it is undergoing a thorough overhaul, and awaiting a more sober paint scheme to replace the rather bright one applied for filming purposes.

Right: *Chance Vought F4U-7 Corsair N33714 pictured in flight over the Californian coast.*
Top: *N33714 wearing US Navy World War II finish for the TV series* Baa-Baa Blacksheep. *However, the F4U-7 did not serve with either the US Navy or Marine Corps. It was the final F4U variant and was produced in 1950, serving with France and Viet Nam; N33714 was operated by the* Aéronavale.

Yakovlev Yak-11 G-AYAK

Alexander Sergeievich Yakovlev's design bureau has been responsible for a wide range of different types of aeroplane, including single-piston-engine fighters, multi-jet fighters, light sporting and aerobatic aircraft, training aircraft, small jet airliners and helicopters. His name first came to prominence with the Yak–1 fighter conceived in response to official specifications laid down in 1938 by the Soviet air ministry. Throughout the war the series was developed, the Yak–7 replacing the Yak–1, and reaching its peak of perfection with the Yak–9 of 1943. The Yak–3 was a lightweight, low-level interceptor, developed from the Yak–1. A S Yakovlev was also responsible for the first Russian jet fighter to enter squadron service, the Yak–15.

In 1946 Yakovlev designed a new tandem-seat, advanced trainer for the Soviet air force, the Yak–11, powered by a 730hp Shvetsov ASh–21 radial engine. The tandem-seat cockpit and ASh–21 were combined with the wings, tail-unit and undercarriage of the Yak–3 fighter. It had a maximum speed of 286mph. Since the 1930s most Soviet fighters have been produced as tandem-seat trainers. Over 3850 were built between 1946 and 1956, some of which were supplied to Communist bloc and Arab air forces. It was dependent upon compressed air for the operation of all its servo-systems, including starting. The short, light wings and the concentration of weight in the fuselage gave it a spectacular rate of roll and, by the same token, power in vertical manoeuvres.

The Yak–11 tandem-seat trainer was also built by Strojviny Privni Petiletsky in Czechoslovakia as the C–11, and in 1964 twenty were ferried to Egypt. While *en route* from Bratislava to Cairo, on March 27 over Cyprus one of these, OK–WIE, developed an engine fault, and made a forced landing on Morphu beach near Philia, in the north-west of the island. Apparently unclaimed by its owners, it became the property of an enterprising garage owner of Famagusta, who put it on his forecourt to attract custom. In 1970 it was discovered by an English businessman, who purchased it and shipped it home.

Registered appropriately G-AYAK, it was delivered into the capable hands of Doug Bianchi's Personal Plane Services, at Booker Aerodrome, near High Wycombe. Engineer Joe Austin, working with very little technical data, over a period of about two years, finally restored the aeroplane to flying condition, painted in Soviet camouflage and markings. In June 1972 Neil Williams, who had often flown in competition against the Yak–18 aerobatic machines of the Russian team, test flew it.

Since then it has become a regular feature of air displays, originally flown with vigour by Williams, until his tragic death in a flying accident in 1977 while ferrying a CASA 2.111 from Spain. G-AYAK was unique as a privately owned, airworthy Soviet military aircraft in the West, if not the world. There are many anecdotes concerning the Yak. On one occasion Neil Williams was flying out to an airshow, and when the huge Shvetsov suddenly began to vibrate heavily, he was forced to seek the nearest practical landing place. This happened to be a USAF base, where they were most apprehensive when they perceived a drab painted but exotic looking aeroplane in the circuit, which not only looked distinctly eastern but displayed Soviet red stars on its upper surfaces. It is said that Williams' protestations of innocence were to no avail and he disembarked, not only to find a propeller tip missing, but to be confronted by the muzzles of a hostile circle of M.16 carbines. On another occasion when the time came for the Yak to take off to perform in an airshow, the ground equipment compressed air bottle was found to be missing, which of course meant that the aeroplane could not be started. Ever resourceful, the groundcrew were able to borrow a bottle from the local police diver and the show went on.

The Yak has been a popular item for a number of years, and its reliability is such that the complete lack of spares and information this side of the 'iron curtain' only rarely causes a problem. On one occasion at the Paris Air show, Doug Bianchi did, however, feel the need to chat up someone in the Yakovlev team, but was amazed to find that there was no way that he could possibly have a Yak–11 in England! Russian aircraft just did not go astray! Moreover, official enquiries elicited the response that no aircraft with the quoted serial numbers had ever been built or served in the Soviet bloc.

G-AYAK was bought by Anthony Hutton in 1980 from Philip Mann, who had owned it for some years. At the same time, a second Yak–11, flown to Israel from Egypt in the mid-1960s, was undergoing ground taxi-ing runs, prior to flight testing. Owned by Robert Lamplough this one (original serial 171101) bears the registration G-KYAK, and probably came from the same batch despatched in 1964 as G-AYAK.

Yak–11 G-AYAK emerged in 1980 in new colours; those of the French-manned Normandie-Niemen Escadrille *which fought with the Russians flying the Yak–3.*

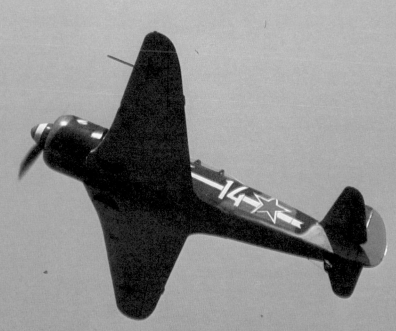

Aircraft Collections

The following section comprises short accounts of some of the more well-known collections and organisations devoted to keeping old aeroplanes flying. Some, like the Salis Collection in France and the Shuttleworth Collection in Britain grew out of the personal interest of individuals, and have become living museums with a permanent home. Others consist of a group of owners and pilots who banded together with a common objective, like the **Vintage Aircraft Club** which was formed in the early 1960s at Elstree Aerodrome, Hertfordshire, UK, as a spontaneous reaction to the rapid and accelerating disappearance of wood and fabric light aircraft in the face of the Transatlantic invasion of easily maintained metal cabin craft. It is as a direct result of such timely intervention that so many of the classic British designs have survived. A similar organisation to the Vintage Aircraft Club, the **KZ and Veteranfly Klubben** uphold the same cause in Denmark, and they too promote fly-ins and a wide variety of social activities, which are open to the usual band of non-flying members, prop-swingers, photographers and enthusiasts.

In North America there is a particular penchant for ex-military machines, particularly of the World War II period. The declared aims of the **Canadian Warplane Heritage,** based at Hamilton Civic Airport, Ontario pin-point the primary concerns of several similar groups, both in Canada and the USA:

1   To acquire a complete collection of World War II and Korean conflict training and combat aircraft flown by Canadians.

2   To develop facilities to display these aircraft.

3   To provide the necessary maintenance programmes to keep these aircraft in flying condition for as many years as possible.

4   To establish an organisation having the dedication, enthusiasm, and *Esprit de Corps* necessary to operate, maintain, and preserve these aircraft.

Membership for the non-owner non-flyer can involve sponsorship of a particular aeroplane and formal commission as an 'officer'. If, as with the Canadian Warplane Heritage, and the Confederate

Air Force in the United States, it is a registered foundation, and aircraft are bought for the collection by a group of people or a corporation, this brings tax benefits.

The Canadian Government itself, like the British Government through the RAF Battle of Britain Memorial Flight, maintains some historic aircraft in flying condition. Although it is felt that continuous flying of exhibits from the **National Aeronautical Collection** would, in the end, by the normal requirements of servicing and repair, destroy the complete originality of unique examples, replicas and part-replica/part-original aeroplanes are flown at public displays. Furthermore, all the aircraft on display at Rockliffe, Ontario, are in fact restored to airworthiness, for the benefit of future generations.

Airworthy aeroplanes likely to be seen flying at

The Canadian Warplane Heritage are: Vought FG–1D Corsair; North American B–25J Mitchell; Grumman TBM–3E Avenger; North American AT–6 Harvard; de Havilland DHC–1 Chipmunk; de Havilland DH82 Tiger Moth; Fleet Fawn.

The Duxford Aviation Society and Imperial War Museum Collection, Duxford, Cambridgeshire, UK

The famous airfield at Duxford, built during World War I and from 1924 onwards one of the most prestigious fighter stations of the RAF, and for two years of the US Eighth Air Force, was at last abandoned in 1963. During the next five or six years the fate of the site was uncertain; a regional sports and recreation ground and a couple of prisons were amongst ideas put forward, and rejected after public enquiries. While the arguments were still going on the then deputy director of the Imperial War Museum (IWM), Dr Chris Rhodes, who quite fortuitously lived in Cambridge, became aware of the existence of the **East Anglian Aviation Society** (EAAS), and when the IWM negotiated the temporary use of one

Arado Ar 396 built by SIPA in France as an S121, visiting Old Warden from the Jean Salis Collection on 30 May 1976. It crashed in 1978

The FAA Historic Flight's de Havilland DH 82A Tiger Moth R9191, at a Biggin Hill airshow wearing World War II FAA trainer camouflage.

hangar at Duxford in order to house some of its reserve collection of aircraft, the two concerns found themselves sharing it.

Gradually, as the other schemes for the airfield fell by the wayside the IWM formulated definite plans to take over the whole site to house all its reserve collection of aeroplanes, vehicles and naval exhibits. By 1975 most of this was accomplished. At this point serious disagreements arose amongst the members of the EAAS and between some of them and the IWM, but the outcome, based on the high regard the national institution held for the workmanship of the independent society, was the formation of the Duxford Aviation Society. It has been enrolled as a Corporate Friend of the IWM with whom it works in close co-operation. It extends its expertise in the maintenance, restoration and preservation of aircraft beyond the exhibits of the Museum and its own collection to the owners of private vintage aircraft such as B–17 Ltd with Ted White's Boeing B–17G Fortress, and to collections like the Shuttleworth Trust. Among its members are highly skilled aviation engineers who, themselves volunteers, head and organise working parties usually assigned to a particular aircraft and have proved themselves capable of restoration jobs right up to full airworthiness, for example, that of Shuttleworth's Supermarine Spitfire Mk VC.

When the M14 Cambridge western by-pass carved away a significant part of the runway the Cambridgeshire County Council became the third interested party in Duxford airfield. The Council secured what was left of the runway, and by a co-operative agreement was able to leave much of the character of the airfield intact. It is the intention of all three parties to encourage the use of the airfield by vintage and light plane owners as a flying base, and the regular shows and open days feature not only visiting aircraft but many airworthy historic machines which are privately owned, based at Duxford.

Very closely linked with the Duxford Aviation Society is the Duxford-based **Russavia Collection.** This was started by Mike Russell and is a sub-group of the DAS. Its main concern is with vintage gliders which Mike and a group of friends from the DAS spend their free time restoring back to flying condition. In addition to this rare collection of gliders, the Russavia Collection is also becoming involved with powered flight. The Miles Gemini is part of the Collection and in addition there is a DH82 Tiger Moth used for glider towing. Two rebuilds are also in the pipeline: a DH53 Humming Bird is being rebuilt with the help of the staff and apprentices at British Aerospace, Aspic Manor, Hatfield, and there are plans to rebuild a de Havilland DH83 Fox Moth.

Fleet Air Arm Historic Flight, RNAS Yeovilton, Somerset, UK

The last airworthy Fairey Swordfish, a Mark II, was already based at Royal Naval Air Station Yeovilton when Chief Petty Officer Gourlay was posted there in 1971. June of that year saw the arrival of a Hawker Sea Fury FB Mk 11 and it was CPO Gourlay who did most of the necessary tinkering to restore it to airworthiness, thus fulfilling the Navy's commitment to its donor, Hawker Siddeley Aviation. By February 1972 the Sea Fury was flying, and the Navy subsequently offered the CPO the job of looking after it permanently. He liked the idea, and persuaded the Fleet Air Arm's museum to lend him their Fairey Firefly Mk 5 which he started to rebuild, with the intention that it too should fly. His new Commanding Officer, Captain Leppard, was himself an ex-Firefly pilot, and CPO Gourlay soon found himself with three airworthy veterans to maintain and a rapidly expanding list of social engagements to which they were invited. He was now 'The Historic Flight'.

Today the Flight attends about fifty shows a year, the engagements being carefully planned to make best use of precious flying hours, for a flight to, say, Prestwick, might take five or six hours, so the oldest, most fragile machine would not be likely to attend. The Swordfish is very handy, however, for the extra

Historic Flight personnel, L to R: C.P.O. R. Gourlay Lt P. Chaplin, Sea Fury pilot, Cmdr N. Rankin, Swordfish pilot, with King Hussein of Jordan, Biggin Hill, 22 Sept 1979.

crew space which can be occupied by the necessary groundcrew who might be expected to cope with any minor hiccoughs in the aircraft taking part in a particular display. Maintenance at home is attended to by regular personnel from HMS *Heron* (RNAS Yeovilton) and their established aircrews; each member has his own duties when he is not actually flying with the Flight. The CO of HMS *Heron,* of course, is entitled as a matter of courtesy to fly any of the aeroplanes at his own discretion.

Naturally, there is little problem in finding willing aircrew, but candidates must have fixed-wing and, until recently, piston-engine experience. Familiarisation begins with a course on their DH82A Tiger Moth, from where the 'student' might proceed to either the DHC–1 Chipmunk or to the Swordfish, before going on to the Firefly. The Swordfish, like the Tiger Moth, has the advantage of another set of wings, a 'back seat' from which the student can peer over the instructor's shoulder into the pilot's cockpit, and in addition a fairly powerful radial engine, which, until recently, went at least some way towards preparing the unsuspecting novice for the first mind-bending fifteen minute hop behind the 2480hp Bristol Centaurus of the Sea Fury. Since the advent of the Historic Flight's immaculate tandem-seat Sea Fury T Mk 20 trainer things are, however, a bit more civilised in that respect.

Airworthy aeroplane of the FAA Historic Flight are: de Havilland DH 82A Tiger Moth; Fairey Swordfish Mk II; Fairey Firefly AS Mk 5; Hawker Sea Fury F Mk 11; Hawker Sea Fury T Mk 20.

RAF Battle of Britain Memorial Flight, RAF Coningsby, Lincolnshire, UK

In 1957 the Battle of Britain Memorial Flight was founded at Biggin Hill, as an aerial reminder of the history of the service, particularly its 'finest hour'. At that time there were two Supermarine Spitfire LF Mk 16s, two Spitfire PR Mk 19s and a Hawker Hurricane. Owing to the cutback in operational airfields at the time, the Flight was displaced rapidly, first to North Weald, then to Martlesham Heath, Horsham St Faith and to Coltishall in 1964. By this time the LF Mk 16s had been damaged in accidents and were downgraded to gate guardians, one at Biggin Hill, and the other at Bentley Priory, which had been the Headquarters of RAF Fighter Command during World War II. Up to 1959 the Flight had led an annual fly-past over London, but when one of the Spitfire LF Mk 16s force landed on a cricket pitch at Bromley, Kent, the veterans were withdrawn, despite protests, from the Battle of Britain Day celebrations. When one of the PR Mk 19s was grounded at Horsham St Faith the Flight was at its lowest complement.

Once established at the old fighter base at Coltishall, itself famous during the Battle, new life was breathed into the Flight. The British Aircraft Corporation presented a Spitfire MK VB, and a Spitfire Mk IIA joined after the *Battle of Britain* film, two years later, in 1967. In 1972 Hawker Siddeley's last Hawker Hurricane arrived and the Avro Lancaster B Mk I was transferred from RAF Waddington the following year.

Sqn Ldr 'Jacko' Jackson, pilot of the Battle of Britain Flight's Lancaster, below its bomb-day, wearing the Flight's distinctive black overalls.

The Battle of Britain Flight's Lancaster 500 feet over Trafalgar Square en route for the fly-past over the Royal Tournament Parade, July 1976.

The pilots of the Battle of Britain Memorial Flight are all serving officers, who continue normal duties when not flying the historic aeroplanes. They are rigorously re-trained to piston-machines through DHC Chipmunks and the three North American Harvards Mk 2Bs lent to them by the Aircraft and Armament Experimental Establishment at Boscombe Down. First flights on the World War II fighters is normally on a Hurricane, with its wider, more stable undercarriage. Aircrew for the Lancaster is drawn from ex-Handley-Page Hastings or Avro Shackleton crews. The most continuous influence on the aeroplanes comes from the dedicated groundcrew, the NCOs and technicians who are on permanent duty with the Flight. The flying time of the aeroplanes is strictly regulated, and every four years they undergo a major overhaul at RAF Kemble, when the squadron coding of the fighters is repainted to represent a different unit which took part in the Battle of Britain. The present base, where the BBMF has been stationed since 1976, is RAF Coningsby in Lincolnshire. From there the aircraft visit not only RAF shows, but Air Fairs and smaller air displays throughout the UK, and occasionally across the Channel.

The airworthy aeroplanes of the Battle of Britain Memorial Flight are four Supermarine Spitfires (Mks IIA and VB, and two PR Mk 19s), two Hawker Hurricane Mk IIs, and an Avro Lancaster B Mk I.

The Shuttleworth Collection, Old Warden, Bedfordshire, UK

In 1932, at the age of twenty-three, Richard Ormond Shuttleworth inherited his father's estates which had been held in trust for him since his death. With characteristic energy he threw himself into the task of running the property, soon becoming popular and respected by his tenants and staff. Educated at Eton,

Air Comm Allen Wheeler getting out of his DH82A Tiger Moth, restored to its black and red scheme as originally delivered to Brooklands Aviation.

The Shuttleworth Collection's Hawker Afghan Hind displayed when near completion, less wings. It is expected to fly in 1981.

he went on to join the supplementary reserve of the 16th/5th Lancers, and was commissioned in 1930. He was cast in the mould of the sporting English gentleman, and was able to indulge his fascination for mechanics and adventure in motor sports, becoming a successful driver and well-known personality at Brooklands, Castle Donnington, the Isle of Man and on the Continental road-racing circuits. In the late 1920s he learned to fly, and his first aeroplane, a DH60X Hermes Moth, G–EBWD, bought to provide transport to Brooklands, still resides at Old Warden. About this time he became friendly with George Stead, an RAF officer with whom he flew to India in 1933, each flying a diminutive Comper Swift, to enter the Viceroy's Challenge Trophy air race.

Shuttleworth's burgeoning interest in flying was not to be restricted to sport, however; he was a board member of Comper Aircraft Ltd, and formed The Warden Aviation Company operating from Heston and using Old Warden for maintenance. His DH Dragon and three Desoutters were available on charter, and three Comper Swifts and the DH60X Moth on a hire-and-fly basis. An offshoot of this enterprise was Aeronautical Advertising Company Ltd, which was concerned with skywriting and neon signs.

While involved with a civic airport project for Bedford in 1935, Shuttleworth was offered a Blériot Type XI and a 1910 Deperdussin, by a garage proprietor, Mr A E Grimmer, of Ampthill, Bedfordshire. So began a collection which, with the

assistance of his chief engineer, L A Jackson, was to become world famous. Shuttleworth continued to acquire old vehicles and aeroplanes until the outbreak of war, when these went into store and he joined the Royal Air Force Volunteer Reserve.

In 1940 Richard Shuttleworth was killed, night flying in a Fairey Battle, having just completed fighter training and only three days before joining an accident investigation unit commanded by his old friend Group Captain Allen Wheeler. Four years later his mother, Mrs Dorothy Shuttleworth, with the guidance of Wheeler, founded a trust in memory of her son. The Shuttleworth Agricultural College and the Shuttleworth Collection reflect his enthusiasm for farming and estate management and for the history of mechanical transport.

The airfield at Old Warden was kept busy during the war, when Messrs Shrager Brothers Limited moved in to provide servicing for the RAF's light aeroplanes. Shortly after the war ended, L A Jackson returned from the RAF to reopen the maintenance side of Shuttleworth's business and for some years, under the auspices of Alan Wheeler, the collection was available to students and visitors by appointment and the old aircraft visited displays throughout the country.

Shortly after the collection opened its doors to the public on a more regular basis, in 1963, Jackson retired and his place as General Manager was taken by Group Captain David Ogilvy. Under his critical eye the pattern of regular monthly air displays took shape

throughout the flying season. The pilots are a select band of highly qualified experts. Most have RAF backgrounds and several are test pilots in the aviation industry. They tend to specialise on particular aircraft, both for reasons of affection and in order to build up an intimate knowledge of individual flying characteristics. The aeroplanes are flown strictly within their capabilities, never flown to their limits, and rarely exceed three hours in the air per season. Maintenance is in the hands of Chief Engineer Wally Berry and his eight stalwarts, of whom three (with an eye to the future) are apprentices, and they call upon the invaluable aid and knowledge of men who actually served as riggers and fitters on World War I vintage aircraft.

Many of the aeroplanes in the collection are entirely unique, as the last flying examples of their kind in the world, and they are of a wide variety, from the 1910 Deperdussin, World War I military machines, light aircraft from between the wars, to World War II fighters and down to the last piston trainer of the post-war RAF. It was always Richard Shuttleworth's intention that his machines should be fully operational, and as a charitable foundation, the Trust ploughs all the revenue gained from its displays, the museum and its benefactors straight back into the restoration of new acquisitions and the maintenance of the exhibits.

Airworthy aeroplanes likely to be seen at The Shuttleworth Collection are: Auster AOP Mk 9; Avro 504K; Avro Tutor; Blackburn Monoplane; Bristol F2B; de Havilland DH51, DH53, DH60X, DH82A, DH87B, DH94 and DHC-1; Deperdussin Monoplane; English Electric Wren; Gloster Gladiator Mk I; Granger Archeaopteryx; Hawker

Above: *Arrow Active II G–ABVE of the Active Preservation Trust, based at Redhill, Surrey, is a unique aircraft. A frequent air show visitor, it is seen at a Shuttleworth flying day.*

Below: *Recently restored to the British Civil Register, Shuttleworth's Parnall Elf II G–AAIN first flew after restoration in June 1980.*

Tomtit; Hawker Hind; LVG C VI; Miles Hawk Speed Six; Parnall Elf; Percival P56 Provost; RAF SE5A; Sopwith Pup; Supermarine Spitfire Mks VC and XI. Additional types (from Tony Haig-Thomas Collection): de Havilland DH60G, DH80A, DH83, DH85 and DH89A.

The Strathallan Aircraft Collection, Tayside, UK

In 1969 an advertisement in *Flight* magazine caught the eye of Sir William ('Willy') Roberts. Two Supermarine Spitfire T Mk IXs and a Hawker Hurricane, which had been used for the making of the *Battle of Britain* film, were for sale. He had always had a soft spot for the Hurricane which, although it had destroyed more enemy aircraft in the Battle than the Spitfire and had indeed been the backbone of Fighter Command in 1940, was consistently underrated and overshadowed by its sleeker, younger partner in the public eye. Unfortunately, the vendor would not separate the three machines which, incidentally, came with a number of useful spares. So, determined to secure the Hurricane, Roberts found himself with the beginnings of a collection.

He insists that the chain of events which ultimately led to the Strathallan Aircraft Collection, started by accident in this way. Almost immediately one of the Spitfires was sold in Canada to Don Plumb, who has since been killed flying a North American P–51 Mustang. To provide himself with a machine on which to gain the right sort of experience to convert a Private Pilot's Licence (PPL) holder to Hurricane pilot, Sir William next bought a North American Harvard Mk IIB, and subsequently an AT–6, the Harvard's USAAF original. And so the number of machines on the short strip near his home at Tunbridge Wells, Kent, grew. At this time he had no facilities, so the aeroplanes were maintained by Shoreham Aviation Services under Jim Smith.

In 1971 Sir William's brother was tragically killed in a flying accident, and the field from which his brother had operated his modest charter company at Auchterarder became vacant. Strathallan offered a

Above: *Boeing B–17G Flying Fortress* Sally B *of B–17 Ltd pictured in a dispersal area at an air display at its home base of Duxford, in front of the World War II vintage control tower.*

Below: *Strathallan's Westland Lysander Mk I, V9441/G–AZNT, pictured in a hangar at Auchterarder during restoration. It first flew again in Spring 1980.*

3000ft (900m) grass runway and a haven from the constant complaints about noise from his sensitive southern neighbours.

When the aeroplanes moved north to Scotland, Jim Smith moved too, to become head of a dedicated team of five permanent engineers. His relationship with the regional CAA inspectors is excellent, backed up by many years of experience and full A, B and C licences on piston engines. The professionals were assisted by an enthusiastic and hardworking Supporters Society. Numbering some one hundred and fifty members, a dozen local to the airfield, they had their own well set-up workshops and took care of the heavy non-airworthiness jobs, such as paint stripping and the neutralising of corrosion, etc. Of direct advantage to the Collection's Avro Lancaster was to be the planned re-alignment and extension of the runway, once a group of archaeologists finished with some unfortunately-positioned henges. The extension would have eased the operation of the collection's de Havilland Mosquito TT Mk 35 which had been grounded since the loss of Neil Williams, who always reckoned the margins of safety to be uncertain.

Sadly, it was announced in autumn 1980 that the Collection was to close, and that many aircraft were to be sold, most it was hoped to new owners in the UK. However, Sir William intended to keep a nucleus of the Collection for his own use.

Airworthy aeroplanes which were owned by The Strathallan Aircraft Collection were: de Havilland DH82A, DH85, DH89A and Mosquito TT Mk 35; GAL 40 Cygnet 2; Hawker Hurricane Mk IIB; Miles M.14a Magister; North American AT–6D Texan; North American AT–16 Harvard Mk IIB; Percival P40 Prentice; Reid and Sigrist RS4 Desford; Westland Lysander Mk III.

Warbirds of Great Britain, Blackbushe Airport, Surrey, UK

Doug Arnold has been at Blackbushe Airport, near Camberley, Surrey, for about fifteen years. It is an old wartime airfield, where charter work, aircraft main-tenance, private and club flying thrive under his auspices. An ex-RAF pilot, Doug Arnold began to think in terms of a collection of warbirds when he flew his own Spitfire LF Mk 16e (Air Ministry serial SL 721, G–BAUP on the Civil Register) for the first time, about eight years ago. Since then he has imported several CASA 352L (licence-built Junkers Ju52/3m) and CASA 2.111 (Heinkel He 111) aircraft from Spain, the latter going on to USA. Always on the look-out for opportunities to increase his

Two Spitfire fuselages in the workshops of Doug Arnold's Warbirds of Great Britain at Blackbushe airport with two volunteers at work.

collection, he has sometimes found it necessary to part-exchange aircraft for the long-term good of the collection. One such painful parting was with his immaculate Spitfire, which was sold in 1977 to American Woodson K. Woods in order to help finance the purchase of no fewer than eight ex-Indian Air Force Spitfires, which are now undergoing restoration under the eye of Chief Engineer Dick Melton, ex-Chief Technician of the RAF Battle of Britain Memorial Flight. Also awaiting treatment is one Messerschmitt Bf 109G, of original German manufacture, rather than the licence-built Hispano HA 1112M–1L variety.

The workshop, which has now been given the official sanction of the CAA, is highly organised, the team working on several similar machines at one time. The Rolls-Royce Merlin and Griffon engines are sent to California to be overhauled, while the airframes are completely dismantled, X-ray tested for metal fatigue, and every corroded magnesium alloy rivet is drilled out carefully and replaced. All metal surfaces are scrupulously stripped and any corrosion killed, and any parts which may be too far gone are duplicated and replaced, before a thorough appli-cation of zinc-chromate. Apart from the full-time engineers, Doug has the welcome assistance of a band of volunteers who refurbish individual parts so perfectly that, once sealed and docketed in polythene bags, the store-room looks more like an annexe of the Spitfire production line at Castle Bromwich than Blackbushe forty years later.

Despite the exemplary quality of the work and Doug Arnold's longtime hopes for a public museum to house his flying exhibits, his efforts to obtain planning permission for a suitable building have so far been to no avail, while American and European parties continue to make attractive offers for the privilege of playing host to his collection. Indeed he has a dozen or more rare warbirds waiting abroad for which he has no accommodation.

There are occasional airshows at Blackbushe when the public have the chance to see some of Arnold's aeroplanes. Recently ferried from the United States, a P–47D and a P–51D have now taken up residence, but perhaps in a year or two a squadron of Spitfires . . .

The airworthy aeroplanes likely to be seen at Warbirds of Great Britain are: Gloster Meteor; Hawker Sea Fury FB Mk 11; Junkers Ju 52/3M (CASA 352L); North American AT–6 Harvard; North American P–51D Mustang; Republic P–47D Thunderbolt; Sopwith Pup; Westland Lysander Mk I.

Antique Airplane Association, Blakesburg, Iowa, USA

Devoted solely to restoring and flying antique aeroplanes, the AAA and the affiliated Air Power Museum, which also flies its exhibits, are based near Blakesburg, Iowa. There is a grass airfield and 1930s style buildings in complete sympathy with the period machines which use it, and a nationwide organisation of 'chapters' and 'type clubs' to assist and serve as local centres to the five thousand or so members. Like so many collections, the AAA started as the brainchild of one man, Robert L Taylor, who in 1953 realised the imminent danger of the complete loss of much of early aviation's material history. With the usual small band of devotees he set about saving old machines from destruction, never losing sight of the fact that the best place for an aeroplane is in the air.

Today the AAA offers a well-structured organisation, operating from Antique Airfield, which pools and disseminates the experience and knowledge of its members through several publications, a technical library and numerous rallies and fly-ins. At Blakesburg there are two annual shows of major proportions, one of which is 'members only' enabling the hard-working owner-flyer-restorer to relax amongst his own kind. Although there are some warbird owners, most of the members fly either inter-war sporting or touring aeroplanes or ex-non-combatant military machines.

The AAA defines 'Antique Airplanes' in categories: aircraft built before World War I (Pioneer);

World War I (1914–18); 1918-37 (Golden Age); 1937–45 (Classic Era); and post World War II, but no longer in production (Neo-classic).

Confederate Air Force, Harlingen, Texas, USA

Probably the largest assembly of airworthy aeroplanes of one epoch in the world can be found at Harlingen International Airport in Texas. The hangars and administrative buildings of the airport's 'Rebel Field' area house a single-minded organisation devoted to the acquisition, restoration and, above all, the flying of every type of World War II aeroplane upon which it can lay its hands. This was not always so, for the original aim of Lloyd Nolan, a wartime flying instructor, and his associates, was to concentrate only on a collection of fighters. In 1951 he was operating a crop-dusting outfit in Mercedes, Texas, and, determined to fly combat aircraft he had missed out on during the war, Nolan bought himself a Curtiss P–40E Kittyhawk. When, six years later, he managed to buy a North American P–51 Mustang which had featured in the film *Battle Hymn* it was at the cost of parting with the other aircraft. Eventually several friends were needed to finance the flying of the Mustang, and the idea of a collection formed amongst a group of mutually supportive flyers and enthusiasts.

By the end of another six years the group had seven fighters scavenged from all over the United States and a couple from Central America. For practical and financial reasons, as well as for reasons of camaraderie, the Confederate Air Force image was confirmed in 1963 as a tax-exempt museum under the command of the mythical Colonel Jethro E Culpeper. A couple of years later the arrival of a Consolidated B–24 Liberator, a Boeing B–17 Fortress and a Douglas A–26 Invader marked not only the formation of a bomber wing, but the end of Mercedes as the home for such a large number of aircraft.

Once settled in at the new International Airport Harlingen, the CAF began to expand in earnest, the flyers of the 'Ghost Squadron' being backed up by over a thousand contributing 'colonels', fifty mechanics and one hundred other personnel.

There is normally a four-day flying display in October, and sometimes a one-day winter event, the former including civil and military acts, the latter devoted to re-enactments of some of the significant battles of World War II.

The airworthy aeroplanes likely to be seen at the Confederate Air Force, including several examples and marks of many of them, are: Beech C–45; Bell

P–39; Bell P–63; Boeing B–17; Boeing B–29; Boeing Stearman N2S–3; Consolidated B–24; Curtiss P–40; Curtiss SB2C; Douglas C–47; Douglas SBD; Douglas A–20; Douglas A–26; Fairchild PT–19; Fairchild PT–26; Grumman TBM; Grumman F4F; Grumman F8F; Lockheed P–29; Lockheed P–38; Martin B–26; North American B–25; North American P–51; North American P–82; North American AT–6; Republic P–47; Ryan PT–22; Vought F4U; Vultee BT–15; Vultee-Stinson L–5; CASA C–2111 (He 111); Hispano HA 1112 (Bf 109); Focke-Wulf Fw 44; Junkers Ju 52/3m; Nord 1002 (Bf 108).

Old Rhinebeck Aerodrome, Hudson Valley, New York, USA

Cole Palen's interest in old aeroplanes started shortly after World War II when he bought a 1929 Viele Monocoupe and subsequently hit the 'Barnstorming' circuit. By 1951 he was in a position to start a collection of antique types and he was lucky to buy up most of the surviving collection at Roosevelt Field, which he had discovered in storage in 1947. Although he continued to fly at state shows and air displays well into the 1960s, since 1958, when he purchased the Hudson Valley farm which was to become Old Rhinebeck Aerodrome, his efforts had been directed more and more towards constructing a home and workshops for his collection. Both restoration of original aircraft and the building of replicas is undertaken.

Today, Palen's background is reflected in his regular weekend shows throughout the summer. In the showman tradition of the Wild West Shows and Barnstorming Aviators most of the flying consists of racing, stunting and cameo dog-fights in a mixture of World War I and inter-war original and replica aeroplanes.

Original airworthy machines likely to be seen at Old Rheinbeck Aerodrome include: Aeronca C–3; Bird CK (1931); Blériot Type XI (1910); Curtiss-Wright Junior (1931); Curtiss JN–4H Jenny (1918); Fleet Finch 16B (1942); Fokker DVII (1918, c/n 286/18); Funk Model B–85C (1939); Gazelle; Piper J–2 Cub (1936); Spartan C–3 (1929); Taylorcraft BC–

65 (1939); Thomas Morse S–4B (1917); Waco O (1926); Waco 10 (1928).

Planes of Fame Museum, Chino Airport, California, USA

The first major aviation museum of the West Coast of America has had no fewer than four homes in its twenty-two years of existence: Claremont, California; Ontario Airport; Buena Park; and finally Chino Airport. The proprietor, Ed Maloney, started collecting interesting bits and pieces of aviation jetsam during World War II, and in 1948 had the foresight to buy a complete Mitsubishi J8M–1 Shusui rocket-powered aeroplane (basically a licence-built Messerschmitt Me 163) which was about to be disposed of as an exhibit in a nearby fairground. It seems difficult to believe now, but, after testing, the US services apparently toured with captured machines for publicity purposes, sometimes dumping whole aircraft when they had fulfilled this role.

Like others during the critical (as far as the preservation of aircraft was concerned) decade after the war, Maloney recognised the need to do something to save examples of aviation's rapid development before it was too late. He opened his museum in 1957 with some fifteen complete airframes, and embarked upon a steady expansion, constantly facing and overcoming partnership and financial troubles, and the need for strategic movement to new premises, quite apart from the obvious personal effort needed to work on his exhibits and put them into flying shape.

Latterly he has of course become involved in the booming interest in vintage aeroplanes and his collection, like those elsewhere in the United States, is constantly changing shape as new machines are acquired, others traded or sold to good homes. The Confederate Air Force purchased a Douglas SBD Dauntless and an SB2C Helldiver and Planes of Fame were able to part with one of only two airworthy World War II Japanese fighters in the world, a Nakajima Ki 84–I–KO Hayate to the President of the Japanese Owner Pilots' Association in 1973, which returned to its home country nearly thirty years after its capture in the Philippines.

Planes of Fame is an independent venture, open to the public seven days a week throughout the summer, weekdays only during winter.

Airworthy aeroplanes to be seen at Planes of Fame are likely to include: Boeing P–12; Boeing P–26A; Convair F–102A; Grumman F6F–5K; Lockheed T–33A; Mitsubishi A6M5; North American O–47A;

Top left: *Confederate Air Force aircraft – Douglas SBD Dauntless, Curtiss SB2C Helldiver, Grumman F8F Bearcat, Grumman F4F Wildcat, Vought F4 Corsair and Grumman TBM Avenger.*
Left: *Confederate Air Force Boeing B–17F Flying Fortress named* Texas Raiders.

North American P–51K; Republic AT12 (2PA); Stinson L–5G; Vought F4U–1.

Warbirds of America, Hales Corner, Wisconsin, USA

Apart from the sheer personal enjoyment of flying a vintage or classic aeroplane, and the personal achievement involved in years of restoration to resurrect one, many owners and pilots admit to a belief that their machines are of a direct historical value to future generations. They would like to think that the flying life of the aeroplane will be longer than their own. Warbirds of America take this angle very seriously, recognising that there must soon be a real scarcity of vintage pilots to fly the vintage planes, and that the occasional tragedy usually comes down to pilot error.

A group of members in California have formed a non-profit-making corporation with the express purpose of providing a safe and structured training programme for aspiring North American P–51 pilots. It cost $2500 to buy into the group originally, and also some five hundred hours' flying time and tailwheel undercarriage experience and familiarity with aircraft of more than 200hp was required.

The North American Texan provides dual flying, and a written and oral examination concludes at least ten hours of tuition. The student must then fly twenty-five hours solo before he has the opportunity to look over the shoulder of a Mustang pilot. The fledgling fighter pilot graduates through tail-up runs across the airfield, through touch-and-go hops until the instructor feels happy to trust him with the rare bird. From the point of view of the collectors it is unfortunate that virtually all flying training today is on nose-wheel aeroplanes so old military trainers are still called upon to provide the service for which they were designed.

The thirty or so members of California Warbirds come under the umbrella of the West Coast branch of Warbirds of America. The national body operates from Hales Corner, Wisconsin, and has become a division of the Experimental Aircraft Association since its founding members decided that they could not handle a nationwide concern properly from California. The more than one thousand members can rely upon a dedicated nucleus of up to fifty volunteers giving time, and sometimes money, when help is needed. Because Warbirds of America consists of individual owners and operators it is not classified as a charitable foundation, and therefore does not qualify for tax-free status in the USA, as does the

Confederate Air Force, for instance.

The concept of Warbirds arose out of the participation of ex-military machines in the National Air Races, which were reborn in Reno in 1964. After World War II, not only had there been a distinct lack of interest in the noisy, fuel-hungry old veterans amongst many private flyers, but the breed had an unfortunate 'cowboy' image that made them slightly alienated at regular vintage fly-ins.

Commander Walt Ohlrich Jnr (now Captain, USN), Bob Love and Ohlrich's crew chief, Bruce Goessling, began to talk about a self-help club for ex-military aeroplane owners. It was obvious from their own experience that everyone was facing similar problems when flying and maintaining the P–51s, AT–6s and B–25s found on the circuits. They were aware of the CAF and when Ohlrich met John Church, an active antique aeroplane enthusiast, the idea of 'Warbirds' began to take shape. In March 1966 Warbirds of America Incorporated was registered in Sacramento, formally and legally chartered by Bob Guildford, a lawyer 'for the owners and operators of World War II aircraft'. The motto of 'Keep 'em Flying', itself a wartime exhortation, now applies not only to combat machines, but to trainers and other aeroplanes of direct military descent.

Jean Salis Collection, La Ferté Alais, Oise, France

Jean-Baptiste Salis bought his first aeroplane with money left to him by his grandmother. He was sixteen, and the aeroplane was a Hanriot Libellule from the bankrupt Clermont-Ferrand Flying School. His first flight at the Champ de Mars ended in a heavy landing which wrecked his landing gear. He graduated to a Blériot Type XI before joining up to win his army wings in 1917. By 1918 Jean-Baptiste was an instructor and by the end of the war had well over a thousand hours flying to his credit.

In 1921 he left the army and set up a repair and assembly shop in Bougival, later moving to Toussus-le-Noble where his collection may already have begun with aeroplanes received in lieu of his service gratuity. His spare time was occupied with display flying both for airshows and films, and restoration work on his old machines. By 1937, when his son Jean was born, Jean-Baptiste bought the Plateau de l'Ardenay at Cerny, near La Ferté Alais, which possessed a natural 2700 foot (823 metres) runway as a private base for his aircraft. The army, who needed an airfield on which to form a school of mechanical engineering, accepted Salis' offer of La Ferté Alais, but had not completed its construction when World

War II broke out. During the war Jean-Baptiste lost all his thirty-three aeroplanes to the Germans.

After the war Cerny–La Ferté Alais became the home of Les Ailes du Sud (Southern Wings) gliding club and flourished, as more clubs formed, until the late 1950s when the encroachment of controlled airspace from the Centre des Essais en Vol (test centre) and Orly Airport began to make serious flying impossible. The gliders had disappeared by 1970.

During these years Jean-Baptiste had been restoring aeroplanes for the Musée de l'Air, Paris, having sold his workshop in Toussus-le-Noble, but he had been lucky in finding a Blériot Type XI, apparently fairly complete, which he succeeded in rebuilding, with the intention of flying the English Channel to commemorate the approaching fiftieth anniversary of Louis Blériot's historic flight in a Type XI. Apparently in order to beat a Canadian rival with the same idea, he decided to do the trip as soon as he could, and in 1954 with only a few hours test flying behind him and his latest (but no doubt familiar) Blériot Type XI the crossing was made. To mark the true anniversary Jean-Baptiste, now sixty-three years old, repeated the flight in 1959. He continued to fly the Blériot in displays until he died in 1967.

When Jean Salis took over he inherited only the Blériot from his father, but in a dozen years had amassed a reported stock of more than one hundred and thirty airframes, a mixture of original, semi-replica, replica and mock (for film purposes), of more than sixty types. Some are airworthy, some are not. The collection remains private, in part funded by Jean Salis Aviation, a company which provides interiors for airliners, although visitors are welcome by prior appointment. There is normally an annual show over a long weekend during the early summer, and smaller displays now and then. Probably as a result of the rapid growth of the collection, and the usual chronic shortage of space, the condition of the exhibits apparently ranges from immaculate reconstruction to stacks of miscellaneous unidentified parts, both under cover and exposed to the elements.

Airworthy original machines to be seen at the Salis Collection include: Blériot Type XI; Bücker Bü–131A Jungmann, and Bü–133A Jungmeister; Fairchild F24 Argus; Leopoldoff; Morane-Saulnier MS130, MS230, and MS341; North American AT–6; Potez Pz60; Salmson Cri-Cri; Stampe SV4; Stinson AT–19 Reliant.

A replica Nieuport Nie 28C–1 of Planes of Fame, painted in the markings of the famous 94th Aero Squadron, American Expeditionary Force.

Aero Engines

It is not possible to go into the details of aircraft engines sufficiently to do justice to them or their designers, but it is possible, however, to introduce the different types which are fitted to the aircraft featured in this book, especially the earlier and rarer engines.

The aircraft industry, right from the very start, has been a perfect example of scientific investigation along with a technological approach to a problem. A cynic might say that aviation did not start its real advance until a quick and easy way of repairing broken bones had been developed, but it was only a coincidence that, in 1852, the Dutch Army surgeon Mathysen discovered the now well-tried method of setting broken limbs by using bandages soaked in plaster. Less than a year later the first man, Sir George Cayley's coachman, was carried aloft in a heavier-than-air machine. There is, in fact, an almost inevitable progression of events leading to the first glider flight and then to the first powered flight. That delay of exactly fifty years between Cayley's coachman being scared out of his wits (he immediately resigned) and the Wright brothers' historic flight was due to the fact that technology had not produced a suitable power source to maintain flight, and it is not unreasonable to suggest that the incredible advances made in the fifty years following the Wrights' flight, compared to the fifty years before it, were due, above all other things, to the rapid development of the internal combustion engine.

One of man's oldest ambitions, it seems, has been to fly, and the full story of flight begins much earlier than 1903. From the mists of antiquity we have the classical myth of Daedalus and Icarus and their wings of feathers and wax. Reliable early beginnings to the history of flight, however, include the kites of the Chinese some 3000 years ago and perhaps their early gunpowder-powered rockets, a mere 1000 years ago. A few hundred years later the airscrew or propeller appeared on the scene in its 'reversed role' on a windmill, developed from the water pumpscrew and waterwheel. Thus the fundamental features of flight — lifting surfaces and propulsion — were known about some 500 years ago.

Leonardo da Vinci features in most histories because of his ornithopter (flapping wing machine) and parachute design, (and, erroneously, his helicopter). However, at this stage flight was mainly theoretical, although optimistic adventurers have for many centuries flung themselves off towers or cliffs in the hope of being able to fly with crude and untried devices, but serious avaiation did not really begin until the first hot air balloon rose into the sky in 1783. Even by that time military uses had been envisaged for 'flying devices' and war time became a growth period for such aviation.

The key to manned flight, however, was the power plant. In 1775 James Watt designed his steam engine and by the end of the century Trevithick was about to introduce a steam-powered, wheeled passenger vehicle. The main means of transport was still the horse, for those who could afford it, or feet, and remained so for several decades, until the introduction of practical steam-powered railway locomotives in the 1830s in Britain. Science was beginning to blossom and gradually during the nineteenth century the theories behind the various external and internal combustion engines were put together. Faraday was establishing the foundations of the electro-magnetic principles without which few modern engines could work and the science of thermodynamics was being developed.

Ten years later, in 1860, the first practical internal combustion engine was built by Lenoir and two years later a four-stroke cycle was developed by Beau du Rochas. The year 1876 saw the introduction of Nikolaus Otto's famous four-stroke petrol engine, the forerunner of most modern engines and the four-stroke cycle has been named after Otto. This was followed a couple of years later by the first engine made by Benz, which was fitted to a tricycle and propelled along at 7mph. The first powered aircraft flew some 25 years later.

It should be remembered that some other forms of transport were only just being developed as well: the 'modern' cycle did not appear until 1865; the first electric rail vehicle in 1835; the electric train in 1879, while the underground railways started in London in 1863. The motor car preceded and has grown up with the aeroplane, though the eventual development of the latter has left the car behind: Benz' motorised tricycle appeared in 1876 and the first Ford car in 1893. Many other aspects of technology were still in their infancy, including metallurgy which is a major aspect of modern aircraft design.

Whilst these developments on the power plant side were taking place, experimentation and research was being undertaken on what might loosely be called the airframe and aerodynamics of flight.

In the mid-nineteenth century the most significant work was being done by the 'father' of English aviation, Sir George Cayley. Born a couple of years before the steam engine had been invented, and long before Stephenson's 'Rocket' steam locomotive appeared, he successfully made a working model of a helicopter and flew a full-size glider monoplane. In 1853 he persuaded his coachman to 'ride' on a full-size triplane glider, and this was the first 'manned' flight in history, some seven years before the first practical internal combustion engine. It was during the years of Cayley's experiments that the ship's propeller, which eventually led to the airscrew, was properly developed. Unfortunately, Cayley died just before the internal combustion engine was built. In the latter years of the nineteenth century many researchers were advancing towards the first powered flight but as yet a feasible engine had not been produced. This was, very roughly, the scene when the twentieth century began and Langley and the Wrights independently strove to become the first men to achieve powered flight.

Many people had been on the brink of flying. Indeed, one or two had actually hopped into the air in their crudely powered machines by the time the Wrights made history. Progress had been slow, but sure. At the time, external combustion engines (steam engines) were also improving, and it has been suggested that if Henry Ford had put a steam engine in his first car in 1893 we would all be driving about today behind steam engines! He didn't, however, and it was the internal combustion engine which began to take over.

The difference between an internal and an external combustion engine is where the fuel, or primary energy source, is burnt. In an external combustion engine, such as a steam engine, it is burnt remotely from the device which actually causes the work to be done; that is, the fuel is burnt under a boiler which produces steam, which is then piped to the actual engine, either a piston or turbine engine, which then converts the energy stored in the steam into useful work. In an internal combustion engine the fuel is burnt inside the actual mechanism which does the useful work, usually immediately above the piston so the hot expanding gases which are the product of the combustion (usually initiated by a spark), can push down on the piston. Mechanical linkages convert the downwards movement of the piston into the rotational movement of a crankshaft which can be made to perform useful work.

Both the Wrights and Professor Samuel Langley and his associates were almost ready to fly in 1902. They had both done their research and designed airframes which, to them, should have flown. The problem was the lack of a suitable engine, and there were fundamental problems to be overcome.

The key to flight

Engines can be made more powerful by making them bigger all over, or by adding more cylinders. This poses very few problems for cars, since the weight of the engine is supported by the road wheels and makes little or no difference to the top speed. The speed is governed partly by the ability of the gearbox to transmit the power efficiently, but mainly by the wind resistance that the car meets. The problem is more complicated for an aircraft because the engine has to create the lift as well as overcome wind resistance, and so if more lift is required because a heavier engine is used, much of the extra power provided by the engine will be used in keeping the extra engine weight in the air and not propelling it along. Thus a good guide to the effectiveness of an engine is its weight to power ratio. This is the weight in pounds for each horsepower generated by the engine. Engine weights vary from about 7 lb/hp to less than 1lb/hp for the most advanced piston engines (in metric terms 1 lb per hp is equal to about 0.61 kg per kilowatts). Jet engines, incidentally, cannot be given horsepower rating as such and comparisons between different jet engines are afforded by the 'static thrust' figure.

At the time in question — 1902 — the weight to power ratio of the available engines were not great enough, so Langley's mechanic Gerald Manly built a rotary engine, and the Wright brothers with their assistant, Charles Taylor, set out to build their own machine. In both cases the whole point of the exercise was to achieve a light, but powerful, engine. The Wrights produced a four-cylinder inline engine which weighed 152 lb and produced a weight to power ratio of 12.7 lb/hp. (While this is the generally accepted figure, Wilbur Wright said in 1911 the engine weighed 'more than 200lb' — attested to by the one-time owners, the London Science Museum.) The Langley/Manly/Balzer five-cylinder rotary engine weighed 187 lb, but produced 52.4hp with a weight to power ratio of 3.6 lb/hp, and could do so for long periods, whereas the Wrights' engine soon overheated. In the event, Langley's 'Aerodrome' was not capable of flight — it was over-complicated and the launching method was too awkward — although Glenn Curtiss flew it, modified, in 1911. It was the Wrights, who had the less sophisticated engine, but the better airframe, who eventually rose into the air.

This in a way highlights another problem: engines get hot, and if they get too hot they cease to function, but to cool them requires extra gadgetry which increases the weight, and so the vicious circle starts up again.

The 35hp Anzani Y engine which powers the Shuttleworth Collection's Deperdussin 1910 Monoplane.

Aircraft engines have evolved into three main types, rotary, radial and inline engines, all working on the familiar four-stroke, or a type of two-stroke cycle, and all having spark plug ignition. The rotary and radial engines are air cooled, and the inline engines can be either air cooled or water cooled.

The Langley/Manly/Balzer engine, although an exceptional rotary engine, died with the rest of the aeroplane and the very first practical engines tended to be radial or inline. Anzani made quite a number of aircraft engines, but only two have been preserved in flying condition. Perhaps the most famous is the 20hp Anzani 'fan', or semi-radial, with three cylinders. This engine made a name for itself by being the one which pulled Blériot across the Channel. It was not a particularly good engine, indeed it has been reported that when Blériot staggered out of his aeroplane his first words were 'More power! — I must get a Gnome.' The Anzani is the engine which is now fitted to the Shuttleworth Blériot. By present-day standards it has one or two rather unusual features. The air-fuel mixture is drawn into the crankcase and as the piston moves down, an automatic valve in the piston head opens, allowing the mixture to pass above the piston for combustion. There is a more or less conventional exhaust valve in the cylinder head, but, in addition, there are rows of small holes at the base of each cylinder. When the piston moves below these holes, the exhaust gases can escape through them, during the short time that the piston is at the bottom of its stroke.

It has been said that the Anzani engine only completed the cross-Channel flight because a shower of rain cooled it. The story is probably apocryphal, but it is quite likely that rather than allowing exhaust gases to escape, the supplementary holes at the cylinder bases served a more useful purpose in allowing fresh, cool air to enter, thus keeping the piston crown cooler. Its weight to power ratio was about 6lb/hp (there is some doubt as to the actual power it was able to develop). A great disadvantage of the fan arrangement was that it resulted in a high

The 50hp Gnome rotary engine fitted to the Shuttleworth Collection's Blackburn Type D Monoplane.

degree of unbalance which would shake the engine apart. This was overcome by a very heavy counter-balanced flywheel, which, of course, again affected the weight to power ratio.

Anzani improved matters with their 35hp radial or 'Y' engine, which powers the Shuttleworth Deperdussin. The symmetrical arrangement of the cylinders results in a much better balancing of the engine, and thus the weight to power ratio was increased to 4lb/hp. The supplementary exhaust holes were also abandoned.

The rotary engine

The 'Gnome' to which Blériot referred and, in fact, fitted to some of his machines, was the 50hp Gnome rotary engine. Designed by the Séguin brothers it revolutionised aero engine design. In a radial engine the cylinders are arranged radially around a circular crankcase and the propeller is attached to the crankshaft, usually directly, the crankcase being fixed to the airframe. In a rotary engine, which superficially looks the same when stationary, the propeller is fixed not to the crankshaft but to the crankcase. The crankshaft is firmly fixed to the airframe and cannot rotate. It is therefore the pistons themselves, in their cylinders, which rotate with the crankcase around the crankshaft and turn the propeller. The idea was not new; it had been put forward by an Australian, Lawrence Hargrave, in 1887, and the American F D Farwell had done some work on one, but it was the Séguin brothers who produced the first practical and exceedingly successful rotary engine, the weight to power ratio being 3.3lb/hp.

This engine still propels the Blackburn Monoplane. The cylinder barrels, including the cooling fins, were machined out of solid nichrome steel, which in 1909 was a very new material. There is a large exposed exhaust valve on each of the seven cylinder heads operated by exposed push-rods. The inlet valve is built into the piston crown itself, similar to the Anzani and, as the piston moves down, the air-fuel mixture, already drawn into the crankcase, passes through an automatic valve into the combustion chamber above the piston. This was not a completely successful method, for the piston crown became exceedingly hot and it has been known for a burnt-out inlet valve to allow the contents of the crankcase to explode! This problem was overcome in the Gnome *Monosoupape* (single valve) by making the air-fuel mixture in the crankcase too rich to be ignited and transferring it to the cylinder by means of a port in the cylinder wall, which was exposed when the piston moved down (similar to a modern 'two-stroke'). In order to get enough air in the mixture for correct ignition to take place, the exhaust valve was kept open for a bit longer than normal to allow fresh air to enter.

As with most of these rotary engines, lubrication is by a total loss system; castor oil is continually fed into the crankcase and gets blown out (usually all over the pilot) with the exhaust gases. Castor oil is used because it does not dissolve in petrol and is therefore not washed off the metal surfaces by the fuel in the crankcase.

Although the rotary engine was very important in the development of aircraft it had its limitations. Cooling was achieved by the rotation of the cylinders in the air stream, creating 'windage', a churning up of the air around the engine which can cause a lot of drag. More important was the gyroscopic effect of the engine and, as the engines became bigger to produce more power, the gyroscopic forces produced by the torque of the massive rotating engine, made the aircraft very difficult to fly. The result of these forces was that when the pilot tried to turn left, the nose dipped and when he tried to turn right, the nose of the aircraft rose, with an engine rotating to the right, or the other way around if the engine rotated in the other direction. The higher the rate of turn, the worse the tendency became.

Rotary engines continued to be developed though many of those in common use were basically Gnome engines, built under licence; Le Rhône and Clerget engines also became popular. The 80hp Le Rhône rotary which is fitted to the Shuttleworth Sopwith Pup can be distinguished from the Gnome rotary by the (usually highly polished) 'pipes' or tubes leading up from the crankcase to the cylinder head. The engine works on a conventional four-stroke cycle (unlike the two-stroke of the Gnome) and the air-fuel mixture enters the cylinder through a poppet inlet valve in the cylinder head. It is drawn into the central collector ring and is taken up to the cylinder head in these tubes. Although this rotary has two 'conven-tional' (inlet and exhaust) valves in the cylinder head it has only one push-rod (or more correctly 'tappet rod') per cylinder to operate both valves. This is done on a push-pull principle, opening one valve on a push and the other on a pull. This means that a special cam is used to operate the 'tappet rod'. This engine had a weight to power ration of 3lb/hp. An 110hp Le Rhône is fitted in Shuttleworth's Avro 504K. The Clerget 130hp, which also had a weight to power ratio of 3lb/hp, differs from the Le Rhône in having a pair of push-rods per cylinder.

Engine control

A major problem with the rotary engine was that the pilot had control only over the slowest and the fastest engine speed. Carburation was primitive. The engines, in effect, were either at full power or off. The early rotary engines, such as the Le Rhônes and Gnomes, fitted to the Sopwith Pup, offered minimal control. The Pup pilot had a petrol fine adjustment lever, which allowed a very fine regulation of the petrol supply flow to the engine, and an air lever, which regulated the amount of air in the combustible air-fuel mixture and was effectively a crude throttle. The setting of this air lever was critical, on a cold day it might be set at the halfway mark, but on hot days the setting would be reduced. Pilot's notes for the Pup state 'theoretically, the position of the fine adjustment lever can be found once and for all for every position of the throttle. . . . Practically, the engine will run this way, but better results are obtained by varying the position of the fine adjust-ment lever with varying position of the throttle. . . .' Lastly, the Pup pilot had an ignition cut-out button, or 'blip switch', located on the control column, which, by cutting the electrical supply briefly, and hence the ignition spark, momentarily cut the engine to control power for landing or taxiing, producing the characteristic 'Brrp-Brrp' sound of the rotary engine, most frequently heard these days emanating from the Shuttleworth's Avro 504.

Later engines, built after 1916, such as the Clerget and Bentley fitted to the Sopwith Camel had elementary carburettors which allowed a greater, but

Top: *8ohp Le Rhône rotary engine which powers the Shuttleworth Collection's Sopwith Pup.*
Right: *A close-up showing the valve gear and crank-case of the Sopwith Pup's 8ohp Le Rhône rotary engine.*

still primitive, measure of control over engine power, and the engine controls remained basically the same. However, the air lever control was improved, and was termed the throttle, facilitated by the improved method of air-fuel mixture induction.

The key to the successful flying of rotary-engined aircraft lies in good engine management, but student pilots found that engine handling was the hardest part of their training, and that the rotary's idiosyncrasies were multifold — and could be fatal. Full engine speed, about 1100rpm was used to take-off and climb, but for normal speed this was reduced by 100–200rpm by decreasing the fuel supply. The lowest adjustment possible was 750rpm but this still gave too much power for low-speed manoeuvres such as landing or taxiing, and the ignition cut-out had to be employed to give the desired power, but often this could only be operated at minimum power.

Although rotary engines were the dominant power plants in World War I, the inadequate control of power was an inherent disadvantage. As the engine power increased, so did the need to control that power, yet the ability to control it was at the same time reduced. This combined with the incredible gyroscopic effects of the heavier, powerful engines made the aircraft almost impossible to handle. Bentley made an impressive 230hp rotary which was fitted to the Sopwith Camel, amongst other aircraft. The curious joint side effects of torque and gyroscope could be put to advantage by an excellent pilot, but lesser mortals had a problem on their hands.

Inline engines

The Germans, at about the same time, tended to go for inline engines. With the noticeable exceptions of the Fokker aircraft which had rotary engines, the majority of the German aeroplanes had Benz or Mercedes six-cylinder, inline, water-cooled engines which were all characterised by the exhaust stack poking up above the upper wing. These are typified by the 230hp Benz which is fitted to Shuttleworth's LVG C VI. A casual glance would suggest that the engine was directly air-cooled, but in fact each cylinder was separately bolted on to the crankcase, and had its own water jacket welded on to it. Each cylinder had two exhaust and two inlet valves operated by push-rods on either side of the engine. The German engines were designed to be built with simple tooling, but by skilled hands, and were intended to be strong and reliable. The nominal weight to power ratio of this engine was 3.6lb/hp.

The plain weight to power ratio can only act as a guide to an engine's suitability for an aircraft and the problem does become more complicated when comparing air-cooled engines with water-cooled engines. Should one take the weight of the cooling water into account, or just the 'dry weight' of the engine? Another important factor is the amount of fuel used. A very thirsty engine might have an excellent basic weight to power ratio, but if it has to be used for long flights, the weight of the fuel must also be taken into account, and this can change the picture dramatically. For instance, comparing two similarly-powered engines of about 250hp, one air-cooled, one water-cooled, but including the weight of cooling water *and* fuel, for an hour's flight the air-cooled engine comes out better at 3.05lb/hp as opposed to 3.84lb/hp for the water-cooled. But, for longer flights the thirstier air-cooled engine has a progressively decreasing power to weight ratio compared to the more frugal water-cooled engine.

British aircraft also used inline, water-cooled engines, characterised by the box-like appearance of the front of the machine due to the radiator being placed immediately behind the propellers. This is evident on the Bristol F2B Fighter, fitted with a Rolls-Royce Falcon engine, and the RAF SE5A, fitted with a Wolseley W.4A Viper engine, giving a 'squared-off' appearance. These engines, unlike the German ones, had the exhaust pipes leading out down the side of the fuselage.

Inline aero engines usually come in two basic forms. One form has a bank of cylinders, more often than not six, which are arranged linearly along the crankcase. There may be a water jacket around them giving the engine the appearance of a modern car engine or they may be air-cooled, having fins around each cylinder. Often the crankcase is on the bottom with the cylinders above, as found in most car engines, but some engines are upside down. The other configuration is the V in which two banks of cylinders are arranged at an angle of about sixty degrees to each other. These are usually water-cooled and may be upright or inverted.

There are two reasons for turning an engine upside down. It is important for the pilot to be able to see

Top: *230hp Benz Bz IX/Bz IV six-cylinder inline engine of the Shuttleworth LVG C VI, showing the characteristic exhaust stack pipe.*
Right: *Characteristic cowlings of the 275hp Rolls-Royce Falcon III engine as seen on the Shuttleworth Bristol F2B Fighter.*

over the engine. Very often an aircraft will be seen taxiing from side to side; this is because the pilot cannot see where he is going, which is not surprising with a tail-dragging aircraft when it is on the ground. However, some aircraft have a severely restricted field of view even when flying because of the position, size and shape of the engine. Alan Chalkley's Comper Swift is a good example of an aircraft with poor forward visibility, especially on the ground, but this is partly due to the parachute seat which positions the pilot lower than normal. The Spitfire as well suffered from a restricted forward view which was most dangerous when landing. To overcome this a curved landing approach was used which enabled the runway to be seen for as long as possible. The other reason for turning the engine upside down is that the line of thrust should be quite high, so that it passes close to the centre of gravity, which means the propeller should be fairly high on the aircraft nose. By inverting an inline engine the line of thrust is raised and the pilot's visibility is improved without having recourse to complicated gearing.

The Shuttleworth Bristol Fighter has a Rolls-Royce Falcon engine. This engine was one of a series of engines, all named after birds of prey, which included the legendary Merlin engine. Rolls-Royce had built the 322hp V12 Eagle engine in 1917, but even before it had gone into production they were working on a scaled-down version, the Falcon. With two banks of six cylinders this water-cooled engine produced 267hp with a weight to power ratio of 2.8lb/hp. This engine also had an epicyclic reduction gear for the propeller. An engine can be made to develop more power by increasing the speed, but if the propeller is fixed directly to the crankshaft this might rotate too fast to be efficient; consequently it became the custom to have high reving engines, but to keep relatively slow propeller speeds by using a gear-box. Early systems used spur gears and tended to be unreliable, so the epicyclic system in this engine was a distinct improvement.

The Shuttleworth RAF SE5A has the Wolseley W.4A Viper V8 water-cooled engine. Unlike the Hispano-Suiza which was also fitted to this type of aircraft, it did not have a reduction gear to the propeller and the thrust-line is lower. The top speeds obtained on the SE5A with each engine were significantly different. Incidentally, one possible advantage of a geared drive which helped to out-weigh the potential unreliability of the extra mechanism was the fact that the position of the propeller

could now be lifted up above the crankcase to enable a machine gun to fire through the centre of the propeller without the need for interrupter gear. It might also be mentioned that one disadvantage of water-cooled engines, as opposed to air-cooled, was that they were more easily crippled by enemy action. A bullet fired into an air-cooled engine might knock some fins off or shatter one cylinder, but the remaining ones could get the aircraft home. However, a bullet in the radiator or water jacket would result in a complete loss of cooling fluid and consequent engine failure.

However, a significant advantage of the inline engine (and radial engine) over the rotary, is that its design permits — indeed demands — the use of a carburation, or fuel-injection, system of great sophistication which gives control of the engine's speed via a throttle, and hence allows fine adjustment of the delivery of power to the propeller.

Radial Engines

The alternative to inline engines was the air-cooled radial engine. These had started with engines such as the Anzani before World War I. The rotary engine dominated air-cooled engines during the war, but as the power began to increase, with the consequent deterioration of handling characteristics as a result of excessive torque, the rotary engines gave way to radials. In Britain the two major manufacturers of these engines were Armstrong Siddeley and Bristol.

The Hawker Tomtit, one of which is owned by the Shuttleworth Collection, is powered by the Armstrong Siddeley Mongoose five-cylinder radial engine. This is not a particularly powerful engine by later radial standards, but it was still a useful and economical engine with a weight to power ratio of 2.7lb/hp. It is also interesting to note that the manufacturers rationalised the design of their engines and many parts were interchangeable between engines in their range. Incidentally, radial engines always have an odd number of cylinders in order to balance the engine. The most characteristic aspect of the Tomtit's engine is its lack of a cowling around it, so that the cylinders are exposed in the air stream, for

Top: *200hp Wolseley W.4A Viper engine which powers the Shuttleworth RAF SE5A is a V-8, cooled by a front-mounted box radiator.*
Right: *Rolls-Royce 640hp Kestrel V-12 engine which is installed in the Shuttleworth Hawker Afghan Hind.*

cooling. This brings up another very important point about engine choice and design. It is very important to have the smallest possible frontal area to the aircraft in order to keep drag to a minimum, and even 'streamlining' has its limitations if the engine has a large frontal area.

This was another advantage of V engines, for, by having the cylinders behind each other the front could be made very compact. Radial engines were, of necessity, large. Research carried out by the National Advisory Committee for Aeronautics (NACA) in the USA, and George A Townend in England, enabled the problem for the most part to be overcome. By putting an annular cowling, with an aerofoil cross-section, around the radial engine the air could be directed over the cylinders to ensure cooling, but, equally important, a fast moving stream of air could be directed along the fuselage, resulting in greatly reduced surface drag, The Townend ring had a shorter chord than the NACA cowling, but the basic ideas were similar. Since their appearance (Townend ring in 1927, and NACA cowling in 1933) nearly all radial-engined aircraft have been fitted with them. In some cases, such as the Gloster Gladiator, the Fairey Swordfish, and Bristol Hercules engines aircraft, this has been combined with the exhaust collector ring into one cowling.

These are not to be confused with the simple cowling around the engines in the Pup and Avro 504K which served more to reduce 'windage' — the churning up of air by the rotary engine — and to contain to some extent the castor oil being flung out by the engine.

Peak Development

The radial and inline engines developed steadily and became more and more sophisticated; supercharging techniques were able to boost the power of the engines and this, coupled with variable pitch and constant speed propellers, raised the operational ceiling of the machines. For instance, the Bristol Mercury engine which powered the Gloster Gladiator, developed 720hp with a weight to power ratio of 1.4lb/hp. This was an incredible improvement over the Mongoose, yet in some ways the engine is conventional, the valves being operated by push-rods, and the extra power being obtained by improved cylinder design, supercharging and higher engine speed, thus requiring a reduction drive to the propeller.

The radial engine came to a peak with the Pratt & Whitney R–2800 Twin Wasp and the Wright R–2600

Cyclone developed in the USA, and the Bristol Centaurus developed in England, during World War II. This latter engine which is fitted to the Hawker Sea Fury, producd 2500hp with a weight to power ratio of 1.1lb/hp. By now Bristols had developed the sleeve valve: rather than having poppet valves in the cylinder head which were opened by complicated mechanical linkage, the pistons moved up and down inside a 'sleeve' fitted inside the cylinder, almost like a movable lining. This sleeve has openings at the top through which the gases can enter or leave the engine. As the engine runs, these sleeves move a short way up and down the cylinder, rotating slightly at the same time, so that at the appropriate moment the hole in the sleeve arrives opposite the hole in the cylinder wall, allowing the transference of gases. The driving mechanism for this engine, though complicated, was simpler than in the poppet valve engines, and resulted in much greater reliability.

Mention must also be made of the legendary Rolls-Royce Merlin engine, once described, perhaps unfairly, as a triumph of development over design. This engine, a twelve-cylinder V, developed from the 880hp Merlin II (with a dry weight to power ratio of 1.6lb/hp), to the 1700hp Merlin 63A engine (with a dry weight to power ratio of .96lb/hp), as fitted to the Spitfire Mk IX. The replacement for the Merlin ws the Rolls-Royce Griffon, which had a greater internal capacity and in its final form could produce over 2300 hp with a dry weight to power ratio of about .9lb/hp or better. By now three-stage super-charging and fuel injection was being used.

There was, of course, always the cooling problem with these inline engines which were liquid-cooled. In the first place, the high operating temperature of these engines meant that water, with its comparatively low boiling point, could not be used for extended periods as a coolant; glycol was therefore substituted. To put a conventional radiator on the front of them was not going to help, but, just as the Townend ring or NACA cowling improved matters for the radial engine, so means were found to cool the inline engine without causing too much drag. The radiators were often fitted in 'scoops' under the

Top: *150hp Armstrong Siddeley Mongoose five-cylinder radial engine of the Shuttleworth Hawker Tomtit.*
Right: *The FAA Memorial Flight's Fairey Swordfish Mk I, showing the 750hp Bristol Pegasus 30 radial and exhaust collector ring.*

engine or wing; initially the idea was to duct the air over the radiator to cool the liquid, and the 'scoop' introduced drag as it protruded into the air stream.

About 1935 it was discovered that if the duct is given the correct internal shape, the air, because it absorbs a considerable amount of heat energy from the engine, can be made to exit at the rear of the duct at considerable speed and thus actually donate a positive thrust to the aircraft. At first these ducts merely served to overcome the drag created by the radiator, but eventually overall net positive thrust could be obtained. This is demonstrated best in the Mosquito. The radiators were situated in the thickened leading edge of the wings between the fuselage and the engines, and as the hot air exited it actually created a measurable thrust on the aircraft.

There are countless reasons behind the success of engines such as the Merlin and the Centaurus. The advances made in fuel technology, the use of better alloys, improved manufacturing techniques, superior ancillary equipment; all these contributed almost as much as the basic design, but eventually the reaction turbine — or jet engine — so overwhelmingly improved the performance of aircraft that, despite advanced design, the high-performance piston engine's days became numbered.

Glossary

Aerodrome S P Langley's name for his flying machine, owing to mis-understanding of Greek. Subsequently, a small civilian airfield (seldom used now).
Aerodynamics Study of the movement of fluids (in this case air), usually in relationship to a solid object, under gravity's influence.
Aerodyne Formerly used for some types of heavier-than-air flying machines.
Aerofoil Body designed to produce lift (e.g. wing) or to have aerodynamic interaction with the air.
Aerofoil Section Aerofoil's cross-section shape, usually that of a wing which, in conjunction with the angle of attack, creates the lift; sometimes named, e.g. 'Clark Y'.
Aeroplane Heavier-than-air flying machine whose lift is created by wings (planes); usually restricted to aircraft with engines.
Ailerons Aerofoil surfaces hinged to trailing edges of wings which control the rolling movement of the aeroplane, keeping the aeroplane in level flight, or, with the rudder, used to turn, or, alone, to bank. The ailerons on opposite wings work in opposition, i.e. the left moves up when the right moves down, tilting the left wing down and the right up. **Ailerons, Frise:** Patented ailerons which try to overcome yaw by using an inset hinge. The aileron's leading edge does not protrude above the wing when the aileron moves down, but protrudes below the wing when it moves up: thus excessive drag is created which helpd to prevent yaw. **Ailerons, Differential:** In modern use, ailerons in which the angle through which one moves up is different from the angle that the other moves down.
Airbrake A hinged surface which can be brought into the airstream round an aircraft to slow it down by increasing the drag. Usually, it can be retracted flush with the surface of the wing or fuselage.
Aircraft Used to describe any form of man-made airborne vehicle including gliders, hot-air balloons or airships, but loosely applied to aeroplanes.
Airfield Operational base for military aircraft, or small civilian airport.
Airfoil See **Aerofoil.**
Airframe The main structure of the aeroplane (fuselage, wings, tail etc.) but not including the powerplant, equipment, systems and armament.
Airscrew Alternative name for a propeller.
Airship Lighter than air, power driven aircraft; normally, a hydrogen or helium filled 'envelope' with underslung control cars, cabins and propulsion units, but possibly a hot air balloon driven through the air by a small propeller.
Airspeed Usually refers to the speed of an aircraft relative to the air through which it is moving. It is highly significant because lift depends upon it. **Indicated Airspeed (IAS)** is the airspeed as measured by the aircraft's instruments and is dependent upon altitude. **True Airspeed (TAS)** is the IAS corrected for altitude. **Rectified Airspeed (RAS)** is IAS corrected for inherent instrument errors.
Amphibian An aircraft equipped to land on and take off from either water or land.
Angle of Attack The angle that the chord of the wing makes with the direction of flow of air towards the wing. At shallow angles of attack the ability of the wing to produce lift is low and thus a higher airspeed is required. As the angle of attack increases lower airspeeds are possible because the lift increases, but so does the induced drag. Eventually at a critical (large) angle of attack the air flow over the upper surface breaks up reducing lift and leading to a stall.
Anhedral (or Droop) Term describing a wing or section of a wing which is angled down from the fuselage (relatively unusual).
Aspect Ratio The ratio of the wing span to width (chord) of a wing; high aspect ratio means a slender wing, as on a glider. Low aspect ratio means a short, wide wing.
Autogyro Trade name applied to Cierva's gyroplane but now applied to any similar machine in which lift is obtained by an unpowered rotor rather than by wings.
Axis An imaginary line through the aircraft about which it may rotate, usually three axes passing through the centre of gravity, one along the length of the fuselage (longitudinal-vertical axis) and a horizontal one (lateral) almost parallel to the wings.
Balancing Planes An early term for ailerons.
Balloon A lighter-than-air aircraft, usually an unpowered spherical envelope filled with hot air, hydrogen or helium.
Banking Inclining an aircraft about the lateral axis, usually during a turn. In this case part of the lift from the wings now provides the centripetal force necessary for the machine to change direction.
Bernouilli's Theorem Explains how lift is achieved, using the principle of conservation of energy. This theorem explains that the pressure of air drops if it is speeded up, and increases if slowed down. Thus, as the design of a wing usually ensures that the flow of air over its upper surface is faster than that under it, the pressure on top is less than that underneath, so there is an overall force upwards, termed lift.
Biplane An aeroplane with two sets of wings, one above the other, often with a slight stagger.
Boundary Layer The layer of air in contact with the surface of the wing which causes drag, i.e. the viscosity of the air is sufficient to hold the aircraft back.
Box-Kite A form of kite; also applied to some early aircraft which, very loosely, resemble a boxkite.
Camber The concave or convex curve of the outer-surface of a wing.
Canard Term applied to aeroplanes which have small wings, and sometimes, elevators, mounted on the fuselage in front of the main wings; they normally replace tail planes.
Cantilever Used when referring to wings which are fixed to the fuselage and have no external bracing or supporting wires.
Centre of Gravity (C of G) The point in an aircraft at which gravity can be taken to act, i.e. if the aircraft is suspended from this point it will be perfectly balanced.
Centre of Lift The point on an aircraft at which all vertical forces opposing gravity can be said to act.
Centre of Pressure The point on a chord at which the resultant lift, represented by a single force generated by the wing section can be said to act.
Centrifugal This word is nearly always used in error when the correct word should have been centripetal (q.v.). Its true meaning is very simply described as an imaginary inertial force.
Centripetal For any object to move in a circle there must be a real, continuous force on that object directed towards the centre of that circle. This is correctly called the centripetal force. Without this force the object would continue moving in a straight line. When an aircraft turns in a horizontal circle it is banked so that the 'lift' from the wings is inclined and the horizontal component of this lift forms the centripetal force. The pilot, too, needs to experience a similar force and this is transmitted to him through his contact with the aircraft, giving the illusion that he is being 'flung out': he is in fact being pushed into the circle by the machine.
Certificate of Airworthiness (C of A) A certificate issued by the Civil Aviation Authority permitting a machine to be flown, and stipulating the operating conditions.
Chord A line drawn through the cross-section of a wing from the leading to the trailing edge; the length of this line.
C/n Constructor's (or contract) number.
Cockpit The compartment from which the aircraft is controlled by the crew (see **Flight Deck**).
Con–Trail Condensation trail, often seen coming from the wing tips of fast moving aircraft, caused by water vapour condensing in the low pressure areas of the wing tip vortices.
Control Column The device used by the pilot to control the elevators and ailerons (see **Joy Stick**).
Control Surface The moveable surface of an aeroplane which controls its attitude in flight, i.e. ailerons, elevators, rudder, flaps, tabs and slots.
Dihedral Used when referring to wings which slope up away from the fuselage making a shallow 'V' when viewed from the front. This configuration gives a degree of stability to the aeroplane.
Dirigible Literally, 'capable of being guided', usually referring to a balloon or airship.
Dive Brake A small retractable surface which can protrude from the wing or fuselage to slow the aircraft down in a dive.
Dorsal Referring to the upper rear surface of a fuselage, e.g. dorsal gun-turret, dorsal fin.
Downwash The downwards deflection of air produced by an aerofoil.
Drag The retarding force created on an aircraft by the air through which it is moving and which has to be opposed by the propulsion system to maintain level flight. **Total Drag** (sometimes called **Profile Drag**) is a combination of **Form Drag**, which is due to the shape of the aircraft, and skin friction (q.v.), which is due to the nature of the outer surface of the aircraft. Sometimes certain aspects of drag are isolated: **Induced Drag** is the drag which must of necessity be created when the lift is generated; **Parasitic Drag** is created by those parts of the aeroplane which do not generate lift; **Wing Drag** is the drag caused by the wings alone; **Interference Drag** is the drag caused by the interaction of the wings with the fuselage etc.
Drone An aircraft, usually obsolete, converted to be remotely controlled for use as a gunnery target.
Droop See **Anhedral.**
Elevator The horizontal control surface which causes the aircraft to climb or descend. Usually hinged to the trailing edges of the tailplane.
Elevon A combined aileron and elevator.
Equilibrium The situation occurring when the drag forces are balanced by the thrust from the engines, and the lift balances with weight of the aircraft.
Exhaust Collector Ring An annular hollow ring fitted round a radial engine into which the gases from the cylinders exhaust. It can considerably improve the cooling and cut down drag.
Fairing A part of the structure of the aircraft specifically designed to reduce drag.
Fan Type Engine A radial engine on which the cylinders take up less than half the frontal circle.
Feathered Refers to the blades of a variable pitch propeller, usually on a failed engine, which have been turned edge on so that the propeller is not turned by the air stream (windmilling) which would result in increased drag and engine damage.
Fin The fixed vertical aerofoil usually at the rear of the aircraft which provides lateral and directional stability. The rudder is usually hinged to its trailing edge.
Flap A control surface which is designed to produce extra lift and used at low speeds e.g. take off and landing, and at the same time they may also produce extra drag. There are many different and ingenious types. Very often they consist of a hinged lower surface at the trailing edge of the main planes (wing).
Flight Deck The take off and landing deck of an aircraft carrier. Also the cockpit of a large aircraft.
Fluid Collective term for liquids and gases, i.e. substances which continue to deform as long as a shearing stress is applied.
Flyer (Flier) Early word for powered aeroplane, used by Wrights, Cayley and Curtiss.
Flying boat A seaplane in which the fuselage has been developed into a hull on which the aircraft lands, takes off, and floats.
Flying Wing An aircraft which consists almost entirely of a wing, with the engines, passenger space, etc. all contained within the thickness of the wing. There is no noticeable fuselage or tail.
Flying Wires When an aeroplane is in flight, the wings are providing the lift, and the fuselage 'hangs' from them. Flying wires (USA — **Lift Wires**) are used to support the weight of the fuselage during flight.
Fuselage The body of the aeroplane.
G Force The acceleration of gravity — taken as a standard against which to measure other accelerations such as might be created in a turn. A 3G turn is one which requires a centripetal acceleration of three times that of gravity. To produce an acceleration, a force is needed and an object making such a turn will experience a force equivalent to three times its normal weight. Hence the use of the word 'force'. Aircraft are built to withstand these types of imposed forces. If the 'G' force acts on the airframe in the same direction as normal gravity when the aircraft is on the ground it is known as positive G (+G). If it is in the opposite direction it is known as negative G

(—G). An aircraft performing a normal loop experiences increased +G, but an inverted loop (q.v.) subjects the aircraft (and pilot) to —G.

Gap The distance between the sets of wings of a bi-, tri- or multiplane.

Geodetic Aircraft structure designed by Sir Barnes Wallis, initially for airships and later used in the Vickers Wellesley, Wellington and Warwick. It consists of a series of criss-cross metal members forming a basket-like structure. Its great advantages are that it leaves the interior free of major structural obstructions and can withstand considerable combat damage.

Glider An unpowered, fixed-wing aeroplane used for gliding or soaring.

Ground Effect Increase in lift due to modification of the airflow around the wing because of the proximity of the ground.

Ground Loop Taxiing an aircraft in a circle, usually accidentally.

Ground Speed The speed of the aircraft relative to the ground; used in navigation.

Gyroplane A rotorcraft in which the rotors are un owered; in the USA can also refer to a rotorcraft with powered rotors.

Gyroscopic Effect A rotating object tends to resist any attempt to alter its plane of rotation. The larger and the heavier the rotating object and the faster it is spinning, the harder it is to turn. If such rotation is completed there is a superimposed tendency for the plane of rotation to change at right angles to the one which was deliberately brought about. This effect was very marked in the rotary engine with its heavy rotating cylinders. Pilots found that in turning the aircraft one way, the nose would dip, and in turning it the other way the tail would dip. This effectively put a size limit, and hence a power limit, on the rotary engine.

Helicopter A rotorcraft that gets both lift and thrust from engine driven, aerofoil section, rotor blades.

High Wing Monoplane A monoplane which has wings joined to the top of the fuselage.

Horizontal Stabilizer US term for tailplane.

Horn Balance A rudder which has all its surface behind its hinges can require considerable effort from the pilot to move it. In order to reduce fatigue some rudders are made with some of their surface forward of the hinge, the air pushing on this forward part of the rudder helping to turn the rudder.

Incidence, Angle of Now the same as the angle of attack: formerly the same as rigging angle of incidences.

Inset Hinge Balance A balancing system for horizontal control surfaces which works in a manner similar to a horn balanced rudder (see **Horn Balance**). The air acting on the portion forward of the hinge helps to turn the control surface.

Interruptor Gear A mechanism linking the propeller and a machine gun fitted to fire through the propeller arc; it synchronises the machine gun with the rotation of the propeller, thus preventing the gun from firing when the propeller blades are in such a position that the bullet would hit them.

Inline Term applied to an engine in which the pistons are positioned one directly behind the next.

Joy Stick Early slang name for control column.

Kigas Manufacturers of a pump used to prime the cylinders of an internal combustion aero-engine with fuel; used to mean the pump.

King Post The bracing strut above the fuselage to which the rigging wires of monoplanes were fixed.

Kite In aviation terms, the easiest form of flying machine; it is towed into wind and creates lift by the angle of the surfaces to the wind. Also used to refer to an aeroplane (dated, slang).

Knot One nautical mile per hour (1kt/h), or 1.153mph (1,852km/h); aeronautical unit for speed measurement.

Landing Wires Rigging wires which support an aeroplane's wings on the ground.

Lateral Axis Axis of an aeroplane at right angles to the fuselage through the centre of gravity.

Leading Edge The front edge of a wing, or aerofoil, i.e. the edge which meets the oncoming stream of air first.

Lift The force created by the wings which usually acts against gravity; more correctly, the component of the force produced by the aerofoils which is at right angles to the overall flow of air over the aerofoil.

Longeron Longitudinal member of an aeroplane's fuselage across which the ribs are secured.

Longitudinal Axis The axis parallel to the fuselage through the centre of gravity.

Loop An aerobatic manoeuvre in which the machine flies in a vertical circle. **Inside Loop** — (normal) the aircraft usually starts it by pulling into a climb, and the cockpit is always on the inside of the circle. **Outside Loop** — (more difficult) the aircraft starts by going into a dive, and the cockpit is always on the outside of the circle.

Low Wing Monoplane An aeroplane whose wing is fixed to the bottom of the fuselage.

Machine Synonym for aeroplane or aircraft; in a scientific context, any device into which energy is put in order to obtain useful work as the output.

Mach Number Method of relating the speed of an aircraft to the speed of sound, thus Mach 1 represents the speed of sound (760mph at sea level); Mach 2 is twice the speed of sound etc. An aerofoil's characteristics change completely when the speed of the air over them reaches Mach 1. Named after Ernest Mach, a physicist.

Main Plane The wings of an aeroplane; the main lifting surfaces.

Midwing Monoplane A monoplane which has the wings fixed to the centre of fuselage.

Monocoque Construction in which the fuselage skin has the rigidity and strength both to be self-supporting and to support other loads. In practice, weight considerations have meant the introduction of stiffening members. Most modern aircraft are of this construction but the term has more significance for older ones. (See **Stressed Skin.**)

Movable Tips An early expression for ailerons.

Multiplane An aeroplane with more than one set of wings arranged above each other. In practice, reserved for those with more than three (triplane).

NACA National Advisory Committee for Aeronautics (USA).

Nacelle In early usage, an enclosed or faired-in cockpit section; in modern usage, the fairing around an engine.

Negative Dihedral See **Anhedral.**

Oleo Strut An undercarriage shock absorber similar in some respects to a modern car's hydraulic shock absorber. Air provides the resilience, and oil, forced through valves in a piston, provides damping to prevent rebound.

Ornithopter A type of flying machine beloved of the very early pioneers which attempted to obtain lift by flapping wings, mimicking birds. Model ornithopters have flown, but man-carrying ones have often been spectacular failures.

Outrigger A projecting structure to support part of an aeroplane; tends only to be applied to pioneer aircraft, 'boom' being the modern equivalent.

Parasol Monoplane A monoplane which has the wings mounted above and clear of the fuselage.

Payload The money earning, or otherwise useful part of the load carried by an aircraft, as distinct from fuel, crew, etc.

Pitch Simplistically, the angle at which the propeller blades are fixed. The finer the pitch the less thrust is created; if the pitch is increased beyond a critical point the thrust falls off.

Pitot Static Tube(s) Two thin tubes, often protruding from an aircraft's nose or wing leading edge, which compare the 'forward' pressure of the air with the 'sideways' pressure, the difference between them being indicative of the airspeed. In some aircraft the tubes are arranged concentrically.

Plane The wing of an aeroplane; or a colloquial word (tends to be frowned upon) for aeroplane.

Production Model Aircraft built to the final specifications and manufactured under standard conditions.

Pre-Production Model A batch of aircraft often completed and delivered to the customer for evaluation of use before full production commences.

Propeller Now taken to mean the airscrew which provides the thrust for an aircraft. Sometimes used specifically to mean an airscrew which pushes an aircraft along as opposed to a 'tractor' which pulls the aircraft and is the more common arrangement. Modern propellers consist of two or more blades, fixed at a slight angle to a central hub, which have an aerofoil cross-section and are slightly twisted. Thrust is created by the pressure on the forward facing surface being lower than that on the rear surface as a result of the blade rotating through the air; there is thus a net force forwards. A **Constant Speed Propeller** is a variable pitch propeller in which the pitch is varied automatically under differing flying conditions to maintain a constant engine speed. A **Reversible Pitch Propeller** is one on which the pitch can be altered to create negative thrust, whilst maintaining normal direction of rotation, using it to slow the aircraft during landing. The **Propeller Disc** is the space occupied by a rotating propeller. A **Variable Pitch Propeller** is one on which the pitch of the blades can be altered. This may be progressively variable as on a constant speed propeller, or may have only two positions, coarse and fine, fine pitch being used at take off. (See **Pitch.**)

Prototype The first working example (or examples) of a new type, used to investigate problems.

Power-to-Weight Ratio The ratio of the power developed by an engine to its weight. This is of little consequence for automobile engines, but crucial for aircraft engines. (See **Weight-to-Power Ratio.**)

Radial Engine An engine in which the cylinders are arranged in a circle around a common crankshaft on to which the propeller is fixed, directly or through a reduction gear. There may be one or more rows of cylinders.

RAeC Royal Aero Club.

RAE Royal Aircraft Establishment, mainly based at Farnborough, but also at other airfields. Early aircraft produced by the RAE were given the abbreviation RAF: Royal Aircraft Factory.

RAF Royal Air Force, formed 1 April 1918 by merging RFC and RNAS, as independent air arm; previously, Royal Aircraft Factory, Farnborough.

RAeS Royal Aeronautical Society.

Reaction Propulsion A means of creating thrust by forcing gas out of the back of an engine which results in an equal but opposite reaction on the engine and thus on the aircraft. This includes both jet engines and rocket motor.

Rib The structural member of a wing running from leading to trailing edge, usually having aerofoil section shape.

Rigging Used in connection with the methods of supporting the wings of an aeroplane and the system of internal tensioning wires in the fuselage, etc. to give rigidity.

RFC Royal Flying Corps.

RNAS Royal Naval Air Service.

Roll **1:** Any movement about longitudinal axis of an aircraft. **2:** An aerobatic manoeuvre about this axis. **3:** A run, landing run, landing roll (USA).

Rotary Engine An engine which has the cylinders arranged in a circle about the crankshaft, but unlike the radial engine, the crankshaft is attached to the airframe and the propeller is fixed to the crankcase, and the cylinders are rotated about the crankshaft, which remains stationary.

Rotor Two or more long thin aerofoil cross-section blades, fixed to a vertical shaft, which rotate to provide lift.

Rotorcraft An aircraft which employs a rotor, rather than fixed wings to obtain lift; may be an autogyro, gyroplane or helicopter.

Rudder Vertical control surface, usually hinged to the trailing edge of a fin, used to guide an aircraft in the horizontal plane. The **Rudder Bar** is the foot bar or pedals with which the pilot controls the rudder.

Sailplane A glider specifically designed for soaring.

Seaplane Any aeroplane which can land on, and take off from water only.

Sesquiplane A biplane which has one wing less than half (*sesqui*: half) the size of the other one.

Side Curtains Vertical surfaces placed between the wings of early biplanes in an attempt to gain lateral stability.

Skid A wooden rail, forming part of the undercarriage of early aircraft, sometimes protruding in front of the undercarriage wheels to offer protection to the aircrew should the machine tip forward. Tail skids were used on World War I aircraft to support the tail.

Skin Friction Drag caused by air moving over an aeroplane's surface (see **Drag**).

Slat A small auxiliary aerofoil fixed closely in front of the main aerofoil leaving a small gap between the two. (See **Slot**.)

Side Slip The sideways movement of an aeroplane through the air. Modern aircraft do not do this very easily, but with older biplanes with small side area, and virtually no dihedral, side slipping was quite a common way of losing height before landing.

Slipstream Flow of air blown backwards behind a propeller.

Slots Gaps built into the wing, or created by slats, which cause a smooth stream of air to flow over the wing surface, enabling the aeroplane to be flown at slow speeds without stalling. **Handley Page Slots:** a device to overcome the problem of stall at low speeds, developed about 1919, which came into use on many British aircraft after 1928. The leading edge of the wing was fitted with a movable slat, which at low speed was brought forward (initially pilot controlled, later automatically) and created the slot through which an undisturbed stream of air passed over the wings upper surface.

Sound, Speed of About 760mph at sea level, but dependent on temperature. The significance of the speed of sound in aeronautics is that the aerodynamics change completely at speeds over that of sound. Normal aerodynamics assume that air is more or less incompressible, but as the sound barrier is exceeded air has to be treated as a compressible and expandable fluid and a totally new set of aerodynamic principles apply.

Span Distance from one wing tip to the other.

Spar Structural members of a wing running spanwise along its length.

Spin An aerial manoeuvre in which the aircraft descends, whilst rotating, brought about deliberately or accidentally by the failure of the wings to create lift because they are stalled. This resulted in innumerable accidents until the recovery technique was discovered by Lt Wilfred Parke, RN in 1912.

Spinner The streamlined fairing over the hub of the propeller.

Spoiler A projection, usually from a wing surface, designed to break up the airflow to destroy the lift or to slow down the aircraft.

Stability The ability of an aircraft to maintain its attitude in flight, control of which is achieved by means of the control surfaces. The wings and their dihedral provide lateral (or rolling) stability, which is controlled by the ailerons. The fuselage and the fin provide stability about the vertical axis (yaw), controlled by the rudder. The fin and tailplane provide directional stability. The elevators control the longitudinal stability of the aircraft (pitching or looping).

Stagger The amount by which an upper wing of a bi-, tri- or multiplane projects in front of (**positive —**) or behind (**negative —**) the one below it, expressed as a percentage of the gap between the wings.

Stall Loss of lift produced because the airflow has broken up over a wing's upper surface, as a result of too slow an airspeed and too great an angle of attack.

Stick Colloquial term for control column; abbreviation of joy stick.

Streamline The path followed by a particle of air round an object moving through the air, which can be made visible by introducing smoke into the air in a wind tunnel, or by special photographic techniques.

Streamlining: shaping an object which has to move through the air in such a manner that the drag is kept to a minimum. Typically, this would involve the use of pointed fronts and gently rounded curves. It is, however, a much more complex science than one might imagine.

Stressed Skin A now standard type of construction, similar to monocoque, applied to wings and tail surfaces. Instead of relying solely on a wing's spars and ribs to take the loads, the metal skin covering the wing also takes a share of the structural load as well as the aerodynamic loading.

Stringer Longitudinal structural member.

Strut Structural member usually taking a compressive load.

Subsonic Speed Speed lower than that of sound.

Supercharger Device which forces more air into an engine than can be taken in through the basic induction. It becomes necessary when the aircraft is flying very high where the air is thin, or if exceptional power is required from the engine.

Supersonic Speed Speed greater than that of sound.

Tab A small auxiliary control surface which is part of, or associated with a major control surface. A **Balancing Tab** reduces the effort required to make the main control surface move. A **Trim Tab** enables the pilot to set a bias on the controls, to compensate for uneven loading, etc.

Tailplane The fixed horizontal stabilising plane(s) at the rear of the aeroplane. Before the use of trim tabs some aircraft had an adjustable incidence tailplane to compensate for variations in the aeroplane loading.

Tail Unit The rear extremity of an aeroplane consisting of the tailcone, tailplanes, elevator, fin(s) and rudder(s).

Tandem Refers to two-seat aircraft in which one person sits behind the other.

Taper The gradual narrowing of an aerofoil: usually applied to a wing in which the chord length shortens towards the wing tip.

Taxi To drive the aircraft on the ground, or water; not applied to take off or landing runs.

Terminal Velocity The final velocity or speed of a falling body which occurs when the air resistance is equal to the force due to gravity.

Thrust The driving force exerted on an aircraft by its power plant.

Torque The 'turning' effect produced by a rotating shaft; the result of a system of forces which tends to produce rotation.

Townend Ring An annular aerofoil section, developed about 1927, surrounding the engine, working on a principle similar to Handley Page slots, as a means of establishing a smooth airflow around the fuselage or engine in order to reduce drag.

Tractor Propeller A propeller situated in front of its engine; opposite to pusher.

Trailing Edge The rear edge of an aerofoil.

Transonic Speed The speed of an aircraft close to that of sound, where the speed of the air over the surfaces may exceed that of sound at particular points.

Triplane An aeroplane with three sets of wings arranged above each other.

Undercarriage The assembly of wheels, skids, struts and shock absorbers, which support the aeroplane when on the ground; or floats, on water.

Vee (V) Engine An engine which has two banks of inline cylinders, which form a 'V' when viewed from the front.

Ventral Referring to the under-surface of a fuselage.

Venturi Tube A tube (as used in a carburettor) which has a constriction in it at which point the airflow along the tube must speed up as it passes through the smaller diameter, producing a reduction in pressure (see **Bernoulli Theorem**) which can be used to draw petrol into the airstream.

Vortex A rotating airflow such as is generated by the wings of an aircraft, resulting in wing tip vortices, and prime cause of induced drag.

Wash-In An increase in the angle of incidence, or attack, of a wing towards the wing tip.

Wash-Out A decrease in the angle of incidence, or attack, of a wing towards the wing tip. Earlier aeroplanes had one wing with wash-in, the other with wash-out to try to counteract the twisting effect of rotary engines. This is achieved by altering the tension of the rigging wires.

Weight Tare – : weight of an empty aircraft. **All-up –** : maximum operation weight (overall) of an aircraft.

Weight-to-Power Ratio The weight of an engine divided by its power, giving the number of pounds weight of an engine required to produce each horsepower. Used to compare aircraft engines, it is the converse of the power-to-weight ratio, which has a similar purpose.

Windage The churning up of air by the rotation of a rotary engine; although this helps the engine cooling it introduces drag and absorbs engine power.

Wings The main lifting aerofoils of an aeroplane. The lift is created because the upper surface curves more than the lower (i.e. is a greater distance) causing the flow of air across the upper surface to be faster than the lower surface. This means a lower pressure on the upper surface (see **Bernoulli's Theorem**) than on the lower surface, hence there is a net upwards force.

Wing Loading Gross weight of an aeroplane divided by the total wing area.

Wing Warping Before the adoption of ailerons to control roll, some aeroplanes achieved some degree of control by altering the curvature of the wing surface by tensioning or relaxing wires connected from the wings to the king posts above and below the centre section. Wing twisting might be a better description of the process.

Yaw The movement of an aircraft about the vertical axis.

Index

Entries in **bold** type relate to illustrations in colour; those in *italic* relate to black and white illustrations